Wallace Milroy's

MALT WHISKY

ALMANAC

A   TASTER'S   GUIDE

NEIL WILSON PUBLISHING   GLASGOW · SCOTLAND

British Library Cataloguing in Publication Data

Milroy, Wallace, 1932-
      Wallace Milroy's Malt Whisky Almanac
      5th ed.
      1.Scotch Whiskies
      I.Title
      641.2'52

ISBN 1-897784-02-3

Published by:
Neil Wilson Publishing Ltd
11 West Chapelton Crescent
Bearsden
Glasgow
G61 2DE
Scotland
Tel: 041-942-0653

First edition published by Lochar Publishing in July 1986.
Second edition published June 1987.
Reprinted August 1987, January 1988, October 1988
Third edition published September 1989.
Reprinted June, September 1990
Fourth edition published April 1991.
Reprinted August, November 1991, March 1992.
Fifth edition published November 1992.

Edited by Neil Wilson
Designed by Hammond Hammond
Maps by David Langworth

Typeset in Times by Face to Face Design Services, Glasgow
Printed in Great Britain by Scotprint Ltd, Musselburgh

Neil Wilson Publishing Ltd gratefully acknowledges the
assistance of The Keepers of The Quaich in the production of
this work.

CONTENTS

ACKNOWLEDGEMENTS

This edition is the fifth in what I hope will become an ever increasing number. Every edition has won the support of the industry both in kind and in real terms — there are a lot of samples to taste and review! Since the third edition, financial support has been forthcoming from The Keepers of The Quaich who continue to do so with this edition. This organisation is run by Gordon McIntosh who has had very close associations with this book since its inception in 1986. I would like to thank not only Gordon, but also The Keepers, their members and the people who produce whisky in Scotland for all their generous contributions in bringing this fifth edition to fruition.

USEFUL ADDRESSES

The Scotch Whisky
Association
17 Half Moon Street
LONDON W1
Tel: 071-629-4384
Permanent displays on
the workings of a
distillery with models
and audio-visual.
Admission free.

The Scotch Whisky
Heritage Centre
358 Castlehill
The Royal Mile
EDINBURGH
EH1 2NE
Tel: 031-220-0441
Adult admission £3.20,
concessionary rates
available. Audio-visual
guided tours, gift shop.
Open all year, seven
days a week.

The Scotch Malt Whisky
Society
87 Giles Street
LEITH EH6 6BZ
Tel: 031-554-3451
Offering a portfolio of
around 80 cask strength
malts, usually around 60%
and up to 21 years old.
Introductory membership
fee is £40 including a
bottle of malt.

The Malt Whisky
Association
LARGS
Ayrshire
KA30 8BR
Tel: 0475-676376
Membership £12.50 p.a.
Magazine, special offers,
mail order whiskies.

FOREWORD

Although Lord Elgin's tenure of office as Grand Master of The Keepers of the Quaich has come to an end, and I have had the honour of being appointed in his place, this does not mean that the Keepers have in any way changed their views as to the excellent service Wallace Milroy's Malt Whisky Almanac renders to the Scotch whisky industry.

It is not only an informative document, it is also enjoyable to browse through while sipping one (or more) of Scotland's malt whiskies, famous the world over for their individuality, their taste and their powers to promote friendship and understanding.

The Keepers are delighted that there is to be yet another edition of the Almanac and commend it to all lovers of Uisgebeatha.

Sir Iain Tennant
Sir Iain Tennant
Grand Master
Keepers of the Quaich

Innes House
Elgin
July 1992

INTRODUCTION

T
he year 1991 has seen a steady growth in the export trade of single bottled malts with some producers establishing record figures. However the overall picture reflects what has been a very turbulent and trying time in world markets and many distillers will be thankful that healthy stock valuations have kept their balance sheets buoyant.

This fifth edition of The Malt Whisky Almanac, first published in 1986, is a reflection of the confidence of the malt sector and the very real enthusiasm of distillers to promote and heighten the profile of their malt whisky brands. Some 200,000 copies of this book have now been sold with foreign editions available in the USA, Canada, Italy, Japan and Germany and I hope to see further editions in Scandinavia and France before the next edition is in print. I am further delighted that this book can reasonably lay claim to being the largest selling book in my native Scotland since the 'official' bestseller figures do not include non-booktrade sales and as such emphasise the book's broad appeal to the wine and spirits trade, the tourist industry and the corporate promotions market — long may it remain so!

Some interesting facets of information have come to light in the production of this edition. Bladnoch distillery, which was recorded as being in the hands of Gibson International in the last edition, is still firmly in the United Distillers' portfolio while Glenlochy distillery in Fort William is anything but. This distillery, which I reported in the last edition as having such a promising and potentially commercial situation for the tourist industry is now drawing paying visitors since the distillery offices have been converted into a comfortable guest house! A similar development has occurred at Ben Nevis distillery barely one mile distant. Since this distillery passed into Japanese ownership a new reception centre has opened and the spruced-up property is beginning to draw a lot of visitors to the foot of Britain's highest mountain.

Similarly, under the personable and efficient direction of Tommy Thomson, the number of UD distilleries catering for visitors has increased and details are to be found in the Discovering Distilleries booklet published by UD and available widely.Tomatin Distill-

ery's reception centre has just opened and should draw
visitors off the A9 to sample another Japanese-owned malt
from the largest malt whisky distillery in Scotland.
Naturally, the established reception centres continue to
thrive, all recording healthy figures despite the generally
poor state of the tourist industry last season.

Among the activities being actively supported by
some whisky producers are pipe band championships,
heritage in Scotland, business innovation, fell-running,
sailing, shinty, golf, football and the arts. These ever
increasing involvements in the sport, music and culture of
Scotland are to be applauded and I hope other distillers are
able to look at their promotions budgets in a similar light.

Since I have added more information to the distillery
entries in this edition, I feel that a quick review of each
line entry is worthwhile.

1. BRAND/MALT

This indicates whether the malt is a commercially
branded, bottled product or whether it is bottled by
another entity, such as the independent bottlers. If it is
listed as a brand then the home trade label will be
reproduced.

2. DISTILLERY

The name of the distillery which produces the malt,
the address, postcode (where available) and telephone
number are then listed.

3. STATUS

The company which owns the distillery (whether
directly or as a subsidiary) or the licensee is given here. I
have bowed to those licensees who prefer their own name
to be listed here as opposed to that of their parent
company.

4. PRODUCTION STATUS

This indicates if the distillery is operational (whether
seasonally or not), mothballed (i.e in a condition to be
reinstated) closed (i.e still in existence but with a low
probability of ever being reinstated) or defunct (i.e either
in existence, no longer licensed and with no prospect of
reinstatement or simply no longer in existence).

5. RECEPTION CENTRE

If the distillery has facilities to cater for visitors then
I have given as much detail of these as space allows. If the

THE MALT WHISKY PRODUCING REGIONS OF SCOTLAND AND NORTHERN IRELAND

telephone number of the reception centre differs from the distillery, then this is also indicated. Opening hours were as accurate as possible at the time of going to press and please remember that some distilleries are still producing seasonally and may therefore not be on stream when you wish to visit.

6. MALTINGS

This most marvellous of processes can only be witnessed at a small number of distilleries although many still possess their old floor maltings and are putting them to good use as reception centres and the like.

7. ESTABLISHED

As accurately as possible the date of establishment of the distillery is given. In a few cases it may relate to the date when distilling activity was commenced on the site or in the very near locality. Clearly, a large number of distilleries have been rebuilt, expanded and often moved and occasionally the date may not concur with the one the distillers prefer to use on their labels!

8. SOURCE

The current source of distilling water (not process water for cooling etc) is given. I expect a few arguments about this, since some sources are disputed!

9. AGE

The age of the home trade commercial bottling is given with variances for export bottlings noted if necessary.

10. STRENGTH

The strength of the home trade commercial bottling is given with variances for export bottlings if necessary. The figure given is the percentage alcoholic content by volume.

11. SPECIAL BOTTLINGS

If a producer is marketing non-standard bottlings then details (where available) are given.

12. TASTING NOTES

For the future I am currently updating tasting notes expanding on these in plain English so that by the time the sixth edition is in print I hope to have reviewed all the available malts which appear in the book. On the subject of taste I detect a growing movement amongst 'connoisseurs' to report nuances of flavour and style in many malts which, frankly, do little to help the average whisky drinker understand what it is all about. This development will do nothing to educate the average drinker in malt whisky. For it is essentially simple — water, yeast and barley — and its flavour is due to how and when it was distilled, how it was aged and matured — in what, by whom, where and for how long. It's resultant complexity is a joy but I am not convinced that the public require to be led up the adjective strewn garden path beloved of the wine cognoscenti.

13. PERSONAL NOTES

Where space allows you are invited to pencil in your own thoughts on the malt in question.

Finally, a word or two on independent bottlings, which for many are where the real surprises can be found. If the malt is not commercially branded the likelihood is that it is available from the specialist whisky shops and the independent bottlers. Details of these bottlings are on pages 138-140. Those brands which are also available as vintage bottlings from the independent bottlers are listed in the same manner. Incidentally, I am delighted to announce that as we go to press William Cadenhead are about to bottle Allt-a-Bhainne and Braes of Glenlivet at 12 and 13 years respectively and also Strathmill at 12 years old. Full distillery details and tasting notes will appear in the 6th edition.

Wallace Milroy
London
October, 1992

SPEYSIDE

F or many whisky enthusiasts malt whisky is most closely associated with Speyside, but in truth this is only half the story. The strength of the association, however, can be seen from the many distilleries which, although not situated beside the River Spey, make allegiance with it when stating their provenance.

The River Livet has also suffered from the same back-handed compliment and over the years many distillers (even true Speyside producers) claimed to produce 'a Glenlivet', when strictly speaking they were stretching not only the geographical boundaries a bit far, but also the patience of the owners of The Glenlivet Distillery itself. It all goes to show how over the last two centuries 'Speyside' has meant high quality, and today the truth of that statement has not diminished at all.

The trade, however, has always tended to look at the large number of distilleries situated in this area as simply 'Speysides', and for simplicity's sake I have continued with this categorisation for this fifth edition. As you will see from the map over the page, the 'Golden Triangle' really exists, stretching from Elgin over towards Banff and down to the cradle of distilling on Speyside — Dufftown. In this triangle lies the greatest concentration of malt whisky-making apparatus in the world, and to savour the atmosphere here is to realise how important and how dearly distilling is held in the Highlands of Scotland. Follow the 'Whisky Trail' which is clearly signposted in this area and you will see what I mean.

The success of the Speyside distillers and their current profusion is due to the production of illicit whisky. At the end of the 18th Century, the Highland product was in such demand that the 'protected' Lowland markets were infiltrated with the higher quality, smuggled produce of the illicit still. Finally, in 1823, an Act of Parliament betrayed the fact that the Government had at last realised the best way to reduce the illicit trade was to make it attractive for

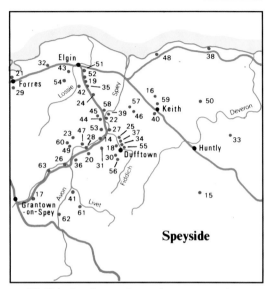

Distillery location numbers refer to page numbers

the distillers to go legal. The Speyside men were, however, suspicious and only after George Smith, who distilled in Glenlivet, went legal in 1824 did they begin to accept the new laws.

Smith's foresight is manifested in the industry on Speyside as it stands today. Famous names abound — Macallan, Cardhu, Linkwood, Glenfiddich, Mortlach, Tamdhu — each and every one another experience to savour. Most of these distilleries now cater for visitors in a number of ways and many of them have outstanding facilities which will not only make a visit to a typical Speyside distillery something to remember, but should also give a comprehensive (and comprehensible!) introduction to the processes involved in the production of fine malt whisky. Local Tourist Information Centres will be able to give details of their local distilleries with these facilities, but where possible, I have indicated if a distillery can accommodate visitors, and how they can be contacted.

Perhaps one of the most promising developments in Speyside has been the recent acquisition of a couple of distilleries from the industry leader, United Distillers. Where once the product of Knockdhu and Speyburn was a little hard to come by, the new owners, Inver House, are now investing in these malts as never before. This at least is a positive sign when one is reminded of Banff, Glen Mhor, Glen Albyn and the like. Hopefully, the closures are at an end now and while I do not foresee new distilleries being established, I am confident that there will be very few further closures.

Brand	# ABERLOUR
Distillery	Aberlour ABERLOUR Banffshire AB38 9PJ
Status	Campbell Distillers Ltd
Production status	Operational
Reception Centre	Yes.Tel: 0340-871204/0340-871285 Mon-Thu: 09.00-11.00; 13.00-16.00 Fri: 09.00-11.00; 13.00-15.00
Established	1826, rebuilt 1880
Source	Private springs on Ben Rinnes
Age when bottled	10 years
Strength	40%
Special bottlings	1969, 1970 vintages

TASTING NOTES

Nose	Rich, malty aroma.
Taste	A hint of smoke on the palate with a restrained sweetness.
Comments	Increasingly popular after-dinner dram now in French ownership (Pernod-Ricard). A well-balanced Speyside in which many have invested in a personal bottling for the year 2000!

PERSONAL NOTES

Malt	**ARDMORE**
Distillery	Ardmore KENNETHMONT Aberdeenshire AB54 4NH
Telephone	0464-3213
Status	Allied Distillers Ltd
Production status	Operational
Reception Centre	No
Established	1898-9
Source	Springs on Knockandy Hill
TASTING NOTES	*(18 year old, 46%)*
Nose	A light aroma.
Taste	Big, sweet and malty on the palate with a good, crisp finish.
Comments	After-dinner dram. A limited edition bottling is sometimes available from Wm Teacher at 15 years and 45.7%. See also Page 138.

PERSONAL NOTES

SPEYSIDE
SINGLE MALT *SCOTCH WHISKY*

AULTMORE

distillery located between *KEITH* and *BUCKIE* began production in
1897. The name, derived from the *Gaelic*, means *"big burn"*.
Ideal supplies of *water* and *peat* from the *Foggie Moss* made this area
a haunt of *illicit distillers* in the past. *Water* from the *Burn* of
AUCHINDERRAN is now used to produce this *smooth, well balanced
single MALT & SCOTCH WHISKY* with a *mellow* finish.

A G E D **12** Y E A R S

43% vol Distilled & Bottled in *SCOTLAND* AULTMORE DISTILLERY Keith, Banffshire, Scotland. 70 cl

Brand	**AULTMORE**
Distillery	Aultmore KEITH, Banffshire
Status	United Distillers
Production status	Operational
Reception Centre	No
Established	1896
Source	Auchinderran Burn
Age when bottled	12 years
Strength	43%

TASTING NOTES

Nose	A delightful fresh aroma with a sweet hint and a touch of peat.
Taste	Smooth, well-balanced with a mellow, warming finish.
Comments	Now available as a brand and suitable as an after-dinner malt.

PERSONAL NOTES

Brand	**BALMENACH**
Distillery	Balmenach Cromdale GRANTOWN-ON-SPEY Morayshire
Status	United Distillers
Production status	Operational
Reception Centre	No
Established	c1824
Source	Cromdale Burn
Age when bottled	12 years
Strength	43%
TASTING NOTES	*(1972, 40%)*
Nose	Light attractive nutty aroma with a hint of smoke.
Taste	Quite full, a malt to savour with a good firm taste which tends to finish quickly.
Comments	A pre-dinner dram.
PERSONAL NOTES	

Brand	**THE BALVENIE**
Distillery	Balvenie
	DUFFTOWN
	Banffshire
Status	Wm Grant & Sons Ltd
Production status	Operational
Reception Centre	No, but visitors are always welcome. Tel: 0340-20373.
Maltings	Floor maltings
Established	1892
Source	The Robbie Dubh Burn
Age when bottled	The Classic: 12 years minimum
	Founder's Reserve: 10 years minimum.
Strength	The Classic — 43%, Founder's Reserve — 40%, 43% for export.

TASTING NOTES

Nose	Excellent well pronounced aroma.
Taste	Big, distinctive flavour. Almost a liqueur and a very distinct sweet aftertaste.
Comments	A connoisseur's malt for after-dinner. The shape of the bottle should appeal to lovers of cognac!

PERSONAL NOTES

Malt	**BENRIACH**
Distillery	Benriach Longmorn ELGIN Morayshire IV3 3SJ
Telephone	05422-7471
Status	The Seagram Co Ltd
Production status	Operational
Reception Centre	No
Maltings	Yes. One of the few remaining floor maltings in Speyside.
Established	1898. Closed 1900. Re-established 1965.
Source	Local springs
TASTING NOTES	*(21 year old, 46%)*
Nose	Light, sweet and delicate with a hint of fruit.
Taste	A positive taste of sweetness and malt with a gentle mild fruitiness that slowly comes through on the palate.
Comments	A pre-dinner dram. See page 138.

PERSONAL NOTES

SPEYSIDE
SINGLE MALT
SCOTCH WHISKY

BENRINNES

distillery stands on the
northern shoulder of BEN RINNES
700 feet above sea level.
It is ideally located to exploit
the natural advantages of the
area–pure air, peat and
barley and the finest of hill water,
which rises through granite
from springs on the summit
of the mountain. The resulting
single MALT SCOTCH WHISKY,
is rounded and mellow.

AGED 15 YEARS

Distilled & Bottled in SCOTLAND
BENRINNES DISTILLERY
Aberlour Banffshire, Scotland

43% vol 70 cl

Brand	**BENRINNES**
Distillery	Benrinnes ABERLOUR Banffshire
Status	United Distillers
Production status	Operational
Reception Centre	No
Established	c1835
Source	Rowantree and Scurran Burns
Age when bottled	15 years
Strength	43%

TASTING NOTES

Nose	A delightful sweet and flowery aroma.
Taste	Firm, positive with a hint of black-berry fruitiness. It has a liqueur like quality with a clean fresh taste which lingers.
Comments	An excellent after-dinner dram.

PERSONAL NOTES

Malt	# BENROMACH
Distillery	Benromach FORRES Morayshire
Status	United Distillers
Production status	Closed
Reception Centre	No
Established	1898
Source	Chapeltown Springs
TASTING NOTES	*(1970 year old, 40%)*
Nose	Light, delicate and attractive.
Taste	Light and delicate but finishes with a pronounced spirit taste.
Comments	A pre-dinner dram. See page 138.

PERSONAL NOTES

Malt	**CAPERDONICH**
Distillery	Caperdonich ROTHES Morayshire AB38 7BS
Telephone	05422-7471
Status	The Seagram Co Ltd
Production status	Operational
Reception Centre	No
Established	1898. Closed 1902. Re-established 1965.
Source	The Caperdonich Burn
TASTING NOTES	*(14 year old, 46%)*
Nose	A light, very delicate fragrance of peat.
Taste	Medium, slight hint of fruit with a quick smoky finish.
Comments	The distillery is across the road from Glen Grant and used to be called Glen Grant No 2. A pre-dinner dram. See page 139.

PERSONAL NOTES

Brand	**CARDHU** (*Kaar-doo*)
Distillery	Cardhu KNOCKANDO Aberlour Banffshire IV35 7SB
Status	United Distillers
Production status	Operational
Reception Centre	Yes. Tel: 03406-204 09.30-16.30, Easter to October. Saturday and Sunday by appointment. Coffee room, gift shop and conference room.
Established	1824
Source	Two. Springs on the Mannoch Hill or the Lyne Burn.
Age when bottled	12 years
Strength	40%

TASTING NOTES

Nose	A hint of sweetness with an excellent bouquet.
Taste	Smooth, mellow flavour with a delightful long-lasting finish.
Comments	Good after-dinner dram, and a malt which is now one of United Distillers' most prominent and popular.

PERSONAL NOTES

Malt	# COLEBURN
Distillery	Coleburn Longmorn ELGIN Morayshire
Status	United Distillers
Production status	Mothballed
Reception Centre	No
Established	1897
Source	Spring in the Glen of Rothes
TASTING NOTES	*(1972, 40%)*
Nose	Light and flowery.
Taste	Light and pleasant with a well-rounded refreshing aftertaste.
Comments	Acquired by Distillers Company Ltd. in 1930, it is representative of a typical small, two still late Victorian distillery. See page 139.

PERSONAL NOTES

Malt	**CONVALMORE**
Distillery	Convalmore DUFFTOWN Banffshire
Status	United Distillers
Production status	Closed
Reception Centre	No
Established	1894
Source	Springs in the Conval Hills
TASTING NOTES	*(1969, 40%)*
Nose	Light, aromatic — heather aroma.
Taste	Much more on the palate than the nose suggests. A pleasant full roundness which drifts away slowly.
Comments	An after-dinner malt. See page 139.

PERSONAL NOTES

Brand	# CRAGGANMORE
Distillery	Cragganmore BALLINDALLOCH Banffshire AB3 9AB
Status	United Distillers
Production status	Operational
Reception Centre	Yes, but it is very basic. Trade visitors only. Tel: 08072-202
Established	1869-70
Source	The Craggan Burn
Age when bottled	12 years
Strength	40%

TASTING NOTES

Nose	Light, delicate honey nose.
Taste	A refined, well balanced distillate, quite firm with a malty, smoky taste which finishes quickly.
Comments	One of United Distillers' Classic Malt range.

PERSONAL NOTES

Brand	# CRAIGELLACHIE
Distillery	Craigellachie CRAIGELLACHIE Banffshire
Status	United Distillers
Production status	Operational
Reception Centre	No
Established	1891
Source	Little Conval hill
Age when bottled	14 years
Strength	43%

TASTING NOTES

Nose	Pungent, smoky.
Taste	Light-bodied, smoky flavour. More delicate on the palate than the nose suggests. Good character.
Comments	An interesting after-dinner dram.

PERSONAL NOTES

Brand	**DAILUAINE** *(Daal-yewann)*
Distillery	Dailuaine CARRON, Morayshire
Status	United Distillers
Production status	Operational
Reception Centre	No, but visitors are welcome
Established	c1852
Source	Bailliemullich Burn
Age when bottled	16 years
Strength	43%
TASTING NOTES	*(1971, 40%)*
Nose	A mild sweetness which is quite gentle and resembles honeysuckle.
Taste	Robust, full bodied, fruity sweetness which really stimulates the taste buds. Has an excellent balance between refinement and positive assertion of malt.
Comments	An excellent after-dinner dram. See page 139.

PERSONAL NOTES

Malt	**DALLAS DHU** (*Dallas-Doo*)
Distillery	Dallas Dhu FORRES Morayshire
Status	United Distillers
Production status	Closed
Reception Centre	Yes. Tel: 0309-76548
Established	1899. No longer licensed but is being run as a 'living museum'.
Source	Altyre Burn
TASTING NOTES	(*10 year old, 40%*)
Nose	Delicate touch of peat.
Taste	Full-bodied, lingering flavour and smooth aftertaste.
Comments	The entire distillery is now run by Historic Buildings and Monuments and is an excellent place to visit. An after-dinner dram which represents a piece of living history available from the distillery. See page 139.

PERSONAL NOTES

Brand	# DUFFTOWN
Distillery	Dufftown DUFFTOWN Banffshire
Status	United Distillers
Production status	Operational
Reception Centre	No
Established	1896
Source	Jock's Well in the Conval Hills
Age when bottled	15 years
Strength	43%

TASTING NOTES

Nose	Light, flowery, pleasant aroma.
Taste	Good, round, smooth taste which tends to linger on the palate.
Comments	Pre-dinner.

PERSONAL NOTES

Brand	**GLENALLACHIE**
Distillery	Glenallachie ABERLOUR Banffshire
Status	Subsidiary of Ricard International SA
Production status	Mothballed
Reception Centre	No
Established	1967-8
Source	Springs on Ben Rinnes
Age when bottled	12 years
Strength	43%

TASTING NOTES

Nose	Very elegant with a delightful bouquet.
Taste	Smooth bodied with a lovely, light sweet finish. Extremely well balanced.
Comments	Built by W Delmé-Evans for Charles Mackinlay & Co Ltd, this distillery produced one of the most underrated malts in Speyside. Now very rare. Only the previous owner's bottling (label shown) is available from Gordon & MacPhail.

PERSONAL NOTES

PURCHASE.

Malt	**GLENBURGIE**
Distillery	Glenburgie-Glenlivet FORRES Morayshire IV36 OQU
Telephone	03438-5258
Status	Allied Distillers Ltd
Production status	Operational
Reception Centre	No
Established	1829
Source	Local springs
TASTING NOTES	(1968, 40%)
Nose	A fragrant, herbal aroma.
Taste	A light, delicate, aromatic flavour with a pleasant finish.
Comments	A good pre-dinner malt, but only from the independent bottlers. See page 139.

PERSONAL NOTES

Brand	**THE GLENDRONACH**
Distillery	Glendronach Forgue, by HUNTLY Aberdeenshire AB54 6DB
Status	Allied Distillers Ltd
Production status	Operational
Reception Centre	Yes. Tel: 0466-82202. Shop open during office hours. Tours from 10.00-14.00.
Maltings	Floor maltings.
Established	1826
Source	Local springs
Age when bottled	12 years (Original & Sherrywood)
Strength	40%, 43% for export (except Canada)
TASTING NOTES	*(Original)*
Nose	Smooth aroma with a light trace of sweetness.
Taste	Well balanced, lingering on the palate with a delicious, long after-taste.
Comments	A good dram, after-dinner and much sought after.

PERSONAL NOTES

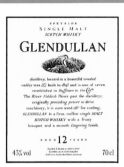

SPEYSIDE
SINGLE MALT
SCOTCH WHISKY

GLENDULLAN

*distillery, located in a beautiful wooded
valley was ⌇ built in 1897 and is one of seven
established in Dufftown in the 19th.
The River Fiddich flows past the distillery;
originally providing power to drive
machinery, it is now used ⌇ for cooling.
GLENDULLAN is a firm, mellow single MALT
SCOTCH WHISKY with a fruity
bouquet and a smooth lingering finish.*

A G E D **12** Y E A R S

43% vol   70 cl

Brand	**GLENDULLAN**
Distillery	Glendullan DUFFTOWN Banffshire
Status	United Distillers
Production status	Operational
Reception Centre	Tel: 0340-20250
Established	1897-8
Source	Springs in the Conval Hills
Age when bottled	12 years
Strength	43%

TASTING NOTES

Nose	Attractive, fruity bouquet.
Taste	Firm, mellow with a delightful finish and a smooth lingering aftertaste.
Comments	Not very well known, but a good after-dinner malt.

PERSONAL NOTES

WHITE HORSE
GLEN ELGIN
SINGLE HIGHLAND MALT
SCOTCH WHISKY

DISTILLED AND BOTTLED IN SCOTLAND
WHITE HORSE DISTILLERS, GLASGOW, SCOTLAND
ウイスキー

| 0 ml | GLEN ELGIN DISTILLERY, ELGIN, MORAYSHIRE | 43% |

Brand	**GLEN ELGIN**
Distillery	Glen Elgin
	Longmorn
	ELGIN
	Morayshire
Status	United Distillers
Production status	Operational
Reception Centre	No
Established	1898-1900
Source	Local springs near Millbuies loch
Age when bottled	12 years
Strength	43%

TASTING NOTES

Nose	Agreeable aroma of heather and honey.
Taste	Medium-weight touch of sweetness which finished smoothly.
Comments	The best of both worlds, an excellent all-round malt, suitable for drinking at any time.

PERSONAL NOTES

Brand	**GLENFARCLAS**
Distillery	Glenfarclas Marypark, BALLINDALLOCH Banffshire
Status	J & G Grant
Production status	Operational
Reception Centre	Yes. Tel: 08072-257. Mon-Fri: 09.00-16.30 all year. Sat: 10.00-16.00, June - Sept. Shop, ship's room, video display, full wheelchair access.
Established	1836
Source	Springs on Ben Rinnes
Age when bottled	8, 10, 12, 15, 21 & 25 years
Strength	8 year old min — 60% ('105') 10 year old — 40% 15 year old — 46% 12 (export), 21 & 25 year old — 43% 1961 decanters

TASTING NOTES	(15 year old, 46%)
Nose	A rich, delicious promise.
Taste	Full of character and flavour. One of the great Highland malts.
Comments	The 60% vol (105°) is an interesting experience, however, not to be undertaken by the unwary! Quoted in the Guinness Book of Records.

PERSONAL NOTES

Brand	**GLENFIDDICH**
Distillery	Glenfiddich DUFFTOWN Banffshire
Status	Wm Grant & Sons Ltd
Production status	Operational
Reception Centre	Yes, very popular with over 100, 000 visitors per year. Tel: 0340-20373
Established	1886-7
Source	The Robbie Dubh spring
Age when bottled	8 years minimum
Strength	40%, 43% for export

TASTING NOTES

Nose	A light, delicate touch of peat.
Taste	Attractive flavour, with an after-sweetness. Well balanced. A good introductory malt.
Comments	If you have never tasted a malt, start with this one.

PERSONAL NOTES

Brand	**GLENGLASSAUGH**
Distillery	Glenglassaugh PORTSOY Banffshire AB45 2SQ
Telephone	0261-42367
Status	The Highland Distilleries Co plc
Production status	Operational
Reception Centre	No
Established	1875
Source	The Glassaugh Spring
Age when bottled	12 years old
Strength	40%, 43% for export

TASTING NOTES

Nose	Light, fresh and delicate.
Taste	Charming, a hint of sweetness which is full of promise with a delicious stimulating follow-through.
Comments	For drinking at anytime. Good to see Highland branding it.

PERSONAL NOTES

Brand	**GLEN GRANT**
Distillery	Glen Grant ROTHES Morayshire AB38 7BS
Telephone	05422-7471
Status	The Seagram Co Ltd
Production status	Operational
Reception Centre	Yes. Tel: 03403-413. From Easter to the end of Sept Mon-Fri: 10.00-16.00 Open on Saturday in July & August: 10.00-16.00
Established	1840
Source	The Caperdonich Well
Age when bottled	UK market — none given. Export market — 5 years old. (Italy), 10 years old and none given
Strength	40%

TASTING NOTES

Nose	Light, dry aroma.
Taste	Dry flavour, light — another good all-round malt.
Comments	Pre-dinner. Hugely popular in Italy with around 70% of the market.

PERSONAL NOTES

Malt	# GLEN KEITH
Distillery	Glen Keith KEITH Banffshire
Status	The Seagram Co Ltd
Production status	Operational
Telephone	05422-7471
Reception Centre	No
Established	1957-60
Source	Balloch Hill springs
TASTING NOTES	*(1965, 40%)*
Nose	A light, dry hint of sweetness with undertones of smoke.
Taste	As with the aroma it has a light, fruity sweetness which results in a smooth well balanced palate.
Comments	Due to its overall lightness both in aroma and taste it is a good pre-dinner dram. See page 139.

PERSONAL NOTES

Brand	**THE GLENLIVET**
Distillery	Glenlivet BALLINDALLOCH Banffshire AB3 9DB
Status	The Seagram Co Ltd
Production status	Operational
Reception Centre	Yes. Tel: 08073-427 Easter to end of October 10.00-16.00. During July and August, open until 20.00.
Established	1824
Source	Josie's Well
Age when bottled	12 & 21 years old
Strength	40%, 43% for export & 21 year old

TASTING NOTES

Nose	A light, delicate nose with lots of fruit.
Taste	Medium-light trace of sweetness, quite full on the palate — a first class malt.
Comments	This one never disappoints. Popular and available everywhere.

PERSONAL NOTES

Brand	**GLENLOSSIE**
Distillery	Glenlossie-Glenlivet
	ELGIN
	Morayshire
Status	United Distillers
Production status	Operational
Reception centre	No
Established	1876
Source	The Bardon Burn
Age when bottled	10 years
Strength	43%

TASTING NOTES

Nose	A soft touch of sweetness with sandalwood overtones
Taste	Has mellowed with age and has a long lasting smoothness with an almond-like finish.
Comments	An after-dinner dram from a remote location near Elgin.

PERSONAL NOTES

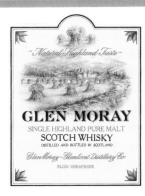

Brand	**GLEN MORAY**
Distillery	Glen Moray
	ELGIN
	Morayshire IV30 1YE
Telephone	0343-542577
Status	Macdonald Martin Distilleries Plc
Production status	Operational
Reception centre	No, but visitors are welcome. Phone in advance
Established	1897
Source	River Lossie
Age when bottled	12 years
Strength	40%
Special bottlings	1960 (26 y.o.), 1962 (24 y.o.) 1966 (26 y.o.), 1967 (25 y.o.). All at 43%

TASTING NOTES

Nose	Fresh, light aroma
Taste	Light, pleasant and malty with a clean finish. A fine all-round malt.
Comments	A pre-dinner dram, beautifully presented in 4 regimental tins — The Black Watch, The Highland Light Infantry, The Queen's Own Cameron Highlanders and The Argyll and Sutherland Highlanders.

PERSONAL NOTES

Brand	**THE GLEN ROTHES**
Distillery	Glenrothes ROTHES Morayshire IV33 7AA
Telephone	03403-248
Status	The Highland Distilleries Co plc
Production status	Operational
Reception Centre	No
Established	1878
Source	Local springs
Age when bottled	12 years old
Strength	43%

TASTING NOTES

Nose	A rich subtle sweetness with a lingering hint of peat-reek.
Taste	A good balance of softness and quality with an exquisite long-lasting flavour.
Comments	After dinner and now available from Berry Bros & Rudd Ltd of *Cutty Sark* fame.

PERSONAL NOTES

Brand	**GLEN SPEY**
Distillery	Glen Spey ROTHES Morayshire
Status	International Distillers & Vintners Ltd
Production status	Operational
Reception Centre	No
Established	c1878
Source	The Doonie Burn
Age when bottled	8 years
Strength	40%

TASTING NOTES

Nose	Light, fragrant and delicate.
Taste	Very smooth and fragrant. A good all-round drink.
Comments	Pre-dinner.

PERSONAL NOTES

Malt	# GLENTAUCHERS
Distillery	Glentauchers MULBEN Banffshire AB55 2YL
Telephone	0524-6272
Status	Allied Distillers Ltd
Production status	Operational
Reception Centre	No
Established	1898
Source	Local springs

TASTING NOTES	*(1979, 40%)*
Nose	Light, sweet aroma.
Taste	Lightly flavoured with a light, dry finish.
Comments	A pre-dinner dram from another distillery founded at the end of the 19th Century. See page 139.

PERSONAL NOTES

Malt	**IMPERIAL**
Distillery	Imperial CARRON Morayshire AB38 7QP
Telephone	03406-276
Status	Allied Distillers Ltd
Production status	Operational
Reception Centre	No
Established	1897
Source	The Ballintomb Burn

TASTING NOTES	*(1979 distillation, 40%)*
Nose	Delightful — rich and smoky.
Taste	Rich and mellow with an absolutely delicious finish. A malt of real character.
Comments	One of the great under-rated malts with a name crying out to be branded. Try it after-dinner. See page 139.

PERSONAL NOTES

Brand	**INCHGOWER**
Distillery	Inchgower BUCKIE Banffshire
Status	United Distillers
Production status	Operational
Reception Centre	Provisional
Established	1871
Source	Springs in the Menduff Hills
Age when bottled	14 years
Strength	43%

TASTING NOTES

Nose	Very distinctive with a pleasant hint of sweetness.
Taste	Good, distinctive flavour finishing with a light sweetness.
Comments	A well balanced malt. After-dinner.

PERSONAL NOTES

Brand	**KNOCKANDO**
Distillery	Knockando KNOCKANDO Morayshire
Status	International Distillers & Vintners Ltd
Production status	Operational
Reception Centre	No
Established	1898
Source	Cardnach spring
Age when bottled	12-15 years
Strength	40%

TASTING NOTES

Nose	Full pleasant aroma of hot butter.
Taste	Medium-bodied with a pleasant syrupy flavour which finishes quite quickly.
Comments	After-dinner. Bottled when it is considered ready, rather than at a pre-determined age. The label carries dates of distillation and bottling, currently 1978 and 1992 respectively.

PERSONAL NOTES

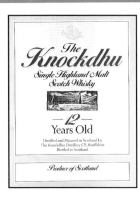

Brand	**KNOCKDHU** (*Knock-doo*)
Distillery	Knockdhu **KNOCK** Aberdeenshire AB5 5LJ
Telephone	046686-223
Status	Knockdhu Distillery Co., Ltd.
Production status	Operational
Reception Centre	No
Established	1893-4
Source	Five springs on the Knock Hill
Age when bottled	12 years
Strength	40%

TASTING NOTES

Nose	A distinctive soft aroma with a hint of smoke.
Taste	Very refined with a mellow smooth, mild softness and a long finish.
Comments	An excellent all round malt. This distillery was the first bought by The Distillers Co to supply malt whisky for their own use. It is soon to be relaunched as *An Cnoc.*

PERSONAL NOTES

Brand	**LINKWOOD**
Distillery	Linkwood ELGIN Morayshire
Telephone	0343-547004
Status	United Distillers
Production status	Operational
Reception Centre	No. Visiting by appointment.
Established	c1824
Source	Springs near Milbuies Loch
Age when bottled	12 years
Strength	43%

TASTING NOTES

Nose	Slightly smoky with a trace of sweetness.
Taste	Full-bodied hint of sweetness.
Comments	One of the best malts available. Don't pass this one by.

PERSONAL NOTES

Brand	**LONGMORN**
Distillery	Longmorn
	ELGIN
	Morayshire IV30 3SJ
Telephone	05422-7471
Status	The Seagram Co Ltd
Production status	Operational
Reception Centre	No
Established	1894-5
Source	Local springs
Age when bottled	15 years
Strength	43%

TASTING NOTES

Nose	A delicious full fragrant bouquet of spirit.
Taste	Full bodied, fleshy, nutty and surprisingly refined.
Comments	A classic after-dinner dram. Outstanding.

PERSONAL NOTES

Brand	**THE MACALLAN**
Distillery	Macallan CRAIGELLACHIE Banffshire
Telephone	0340871-471
Status	The Macallan Distillers PLC
Production status	Operational
Reception Centre	No. Visitors by appointment only. Tours of Easter Elchies House conducted Mon-Fri at 11.00 and 14.00. Distillery is closed to visitors.
Established	c1824
Source	Borehole aquifers
Age when bottled	UK market — 10, 18 (currently 1974 distillation) and 25 years old. Export — 7, 12, 18 and 25yrs. Italian market — 7 years old.
Strength	7 and 10 year old — 40% 12, 18 and 25y.o. bottlings — 43%.

TASTING NOTES	*(10 year old, 40%)*
Nose	Smooth aroma with a silky bouquet.
Taste	Full, delightful and sherried with a beautiful lingering aftertaste.
Comments	Masterpiece. Casked in sherrywood.
PERSONAL NOTES	

Brand	**MILTON DUFF**
Distillery	Miltonduff-Glenlivet
	ELGIN
	Morayshire IV30 3TQ
Telephone	0343-547433
Status	Allied Distillers Ltd
Production status	Operational
Reception Centre	No. Tours are conducted Mon-Thu.
Established	1824
Source	Loch Moray
Age when bottled	12 years
Strength	40%

TASTING NOTES

Nose	Agreeable, fragrant bouquet.
Taste	Medium bodied with a pleasant, well matured, subtle finish.
Comments	After-dinner. Another malt called *Mosstowie* used to be produced from Lomond-type stills at Milton Duff and is available from the independent bottlers.

PERSONAL NOTES

Brand	**MORTLACH**
Distillery	Mortlach DUFFTOWN Banffshire
Status	United Distillers
Production status	Operational
Reception Centre	No
Established	c1823
Source	Springs in the Conval Hills
Age when bottled	16 years
Strength	43%

TASTING NOTES	(15 year old, 40%)
Nose	A pleasant, well rounded aroma.
Taste	Medium bodied with a well balanced delightful finish.
Comments	A first class after-dinner malt.

PERSONAL NOTES

Brand	**PITTYVAICH**
Distillery	Pittyvaich DUFFTOWN Banffshire
Status	United Distillers
Production status	Operational
Reception Centre	No
Established	1974
Source	Two major local springs
Age when botled	12years
Strength	43%

TASTING NOTES

Nose	Rather elegant with a delicate fragrance.
Taste	Mellow and soft with a fulfilling roundness.
Comments	A remarkably good addition to the bottled malts. After dinner.

PERSONAL NOTES

Brand	**THE SINGLETON OF AUCHROISK**
Distillery	Auchroisk MULBEN Banffshire AB55 3XS
Telephone	0542-6333
Status	International Distillers & Vintners Ltd
Production status	Operational
Reception Centre	No. Tours by appointment
Established	1974
Source	Dorie's Well
Age when bottled	10 years minimum, 12 for Japan
Strength	40%, 43% for export

TASTING NOTES

Nose	Distinctive, attractive bouquet with a touch of fruit.
Taste	Medium weight, hint of sweetness with a delicious long-lasting flavour.
Comments	After-dinner. A first-class malt with 7 international gold awards in the last 6 years. The Singleton 'Particular' is available only in Japan.

PERSONAL NOTES

Malt	# SPEYBURN
Distillery	Speyburn ROTHES Morayshire IV33 7AG
Telephone	03403-213
Status	Speyburn-Glenlivet Distillery Co., Ltd.
Production status	Operational
Reception Centre	No
Established	1897
Source	The Granty Burn sourced on the western slope of the Glen of Rothes.

ASTING NOTES	*(1971, 40%)*
Nose	A heather-honey bouquet.
Taste	Big, full-bodied malty taste with a sweet finish.
Comments	After-dinner. Some of the old United Distillers' bottling will still be around before it is branded by the new owners.

PERSONAL NOTES

Brand	**STRATHISLA**
	(*Strath-eyela*)
Distillery	Strathisla
	KEITH
	Banffshire, AB55 3BS
Status	The Seagram Co Ltd
Production status	Operational
Reception Centre	Yes. Tel: 05422-7471 Open from May to end of Sept, Mon-Fri: 09.00-16.00
Established	1786
Source	Fons Bulliens's Well
Age when bottled	12 years
Strength	40%

TASTING NOTES

Nose	Beautiful, bewitching fragrance of fruit which also reflects the taste to come.
Taste	Slender hint of sweetness with an extremely long, lingering fullness. Good balance.
Comments	An excellent after-dinner malt — one of the best to sip and savour. Distilled and bottled by Chivas Brothers Ltd.

PERSONAL NOTES

Brand	**TAMDHU** *(Tamm-doo)*
Distillery	Tamdhu Heathcote House KNOCKANDO Morayshire IV35 7RR
Status	The Highland Distilleries Co plc
Production status	Operational
Reception Centre	Yes. Tel: 03406-221. From Easter to October, Mon-Fri: 10.00-16.00 and Saturdays from June to Sept.
Maltings	Yes. Saladin maltings which supply all the malt requirement.
Established	1896-7
Source	A spring beneath the distillery
Age when bottled	10 & 15 years
Strength	40%; 15 year old — 43%

TASTING NOTES

Nose	Light aroma with a trace of sweetness.
Taste	Medium, with a little sweetness and a very mellow finish.
Comments	A good after-dinner dram which is both popular and readily available.

PERSONAL NOTES

Brand	**TAMNAVULIN**
	(*Tamna-voolin*)
Distillery	Tamnavulin
	BALLINDALLOCH
	Banffshire
Telephone	08073-285
Status	The Invergordon Distillers Group Plc
Production status	Operational
Reception Centre	Yes. A charming old mill with a beautiful sheltered picnic area. Video, hospitality suite and shop.
Established	1965-6
Source	Underground reservoir fed by springs
Age when bottled	10 years
Strength	40%, 43% for export
Special bottlings	Stillman's Dram — a rare 25y.o.

TASTING NOTES

Nose	Well matured with a distinct mellowness and a hint of sweetness.
Taste	Medium weight with a light, smoky, pronounced finish.
Comments	A good all-round malt.

PERSONAL NOTES

STILLANS DRAM
RARE 25 Y.O.

Brand	**TOMINTOUL GLENLIVET** (*Tommin-towl*)
Distillery	Tomintoul-Glenlivet BALLINDALLOCH Banffshire
Telephone	0807-3274
Status	Whyte & Mackay Distillers Ltd
Production status	Operational
Reception Centre	No
Established	1964-5
Source	The Ballantruan Spring
Age when bottled	8, 12 years
Strength	40%, 43% for export

TASTING NOTES

Nose	Light and delicate.
Taste	Light body with good character.
Comments	A good introduction to malt.

PERSONAL NOTES

Brand	# THE TORMORE
Distillery	Tormore Advie, GRANTOWN-ON-SPEY Morayshire PH26 3LR
Telephone	0807-5244
Status	Allied Distillers Ltd
Production status	Operational
Reception Centre	No. By appointment only. Telephone in advance.
Established	1958-60
Source	The Achvochkie Burn
Age when bottled	10 years
Strength	40%, 43% for export

TASTING NOTES

Nose	Nicely defined dry aroma.
Taste	Medium-bodied with a hint of sweetness and a pleasant, lingering aftertaste.
Comments	After-dinner.

PERSONAL NOTES

THE HIGHLANDS

Outwith the Speyside area distilling activity is spread more sparsely throughout a wide area which I have taken the liberty to break up into four main regions in the North, South, East and West.

Over 30 malts emanate from these four areas, some sadly from distilleries no longer in existence such as Glen Mhor, Glen Albyn and Millburn in Inverness, and Glenugie near Peterhead. When you do come across an example of these, remember that you really will be buying a piece of history.

In the far-flung producing localities around the Highlands the importance of the visitor is often keenly felt and despite the travel required to reach these facilities, Highland hospitality still abounds. The existing distilleries in the Northern region stretch from Dalwhinnie near Kingussie to Pulteney at Wick in the north of Caithness and encompass Tomatin at the hamlet of the same name; Royal Brackla near Nairn; Ord Distillery at Muir of Ord in the Black Isle; Dalmore and Teaninich at Alness; Balblair and Glenmorangie near Tain and Clynelish near Brora. Although some of these malts are not as well known as they should be, many are becoming more popular and none of them should be passed by if you come across them.

The Eastern malts lie between the generalised Speyside region and the North Sea coast. Banff, the fishing town on the Moray Firth possesses two distilleries, though only Glen Deveron is currently in production. The distillery with the town's name has been closed for some time and the availability of the malt has fluctuated in the recent past. However, both independent bottlers currently list bottlings of Banff as well as Glenugie which was situated in Peterhead.

Farming has made the lush lowland area around Aberdeen famous, so it is no surprise to find that at Glen Garioch waste heat from the direct-fired stills is used to cultivate tomatoes and pot plants. And while Lochnagar cannot offer the visitor such horticultural

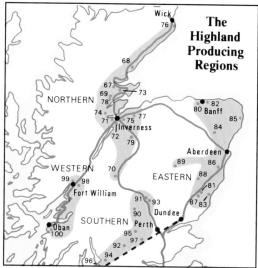

Distillery location numbers refer to page numbers

delights, its successful reception centre and proximity to Balmoral Castle make it not only Royal, but a bit special. To the south of Deeside Glenury Royal near Stonehaven and Fettercairn extend the activity to Montrose which boasts a considerable amount of distilling.

Glenesk distillery has changed names a few times but its malt remains the same whereas Lochside Distillery (once a brewery) produces both grain and malt whisky. Lochside is very rare and I have been unable to sample any of this product to date. Inland, but still on the South Esk river, Brechin has two distilleries at Glencadam and North Port — again both producing quite rare malts. South of this arable region the hills of Perthshire signal the Southern limits of the Highland distilling area.

At Pitlochry, the gateway to the Highlands, the malt drinker can experience two contrasting distilleries. Edradour is the smallest in Scotland and yet maintains all the advantages of a small 19th century plant, while

Blair Athol is a large modern distillery with a
large reception centre and retail outlet. Aberfeldy
Distillery lies at the eastern entrance to the town
of the same name on the banks of the River Tay
and Glenturret Distillery at Crieff caters for the
visitor as well as any distillery can. Tullibardine at
Blackford is a 'recent' distillery (1948) in a village
which not only has a mineral water producer
(Highland Spring) but also the only commercial
malting floors in Scotland built on arguably the
oldest brewery site in Scotland! And if that amount
of diversity is a surprise, Deanston Distillery on
the River Teith at Doune is a converted cotton mill
where the vaulted weaving sheds act as bonded
warehouses and a small hydro-electric generating
station is also situated within the plant itself.

In the far west of this most southerly of the
Highland regions lie Loch Lomond and Glengoyne
distilleries. Both almost straddle the Highland line (as
does Tullibardine) but claim allegiance to the
Highland region. Loch Lomond is a relatively new
distillery (1968) which currently produces Inchmurrin
malt, whereas Glengoyne has a longer pedigree and
resting in a cleft of the Campsie Fells, uniquely caters
for visitors with guided tours, retail outlet and a bar
with a balcony overlooking a rock pool.

The Western malts are an altogether rarer breed
being only three in number. Oban's distillery is
situated just off the High Street of this thriving tourist
town and is therefore extremely accessible for the
visitor. Ben Nevis Distillery in Fort William is in
good health and is most aptly named considering the
breathtaking backdrop. Its neighbour, Glen Lochy
will sadly become a rare malt since the distillery is
now closed for good.

THE NORTHERN HIGHLANDS

Brand	**BALBLAIR**
Distillery	Balblair Edderton
	TAIN
	Ross-shire IV19 1LB
Telephone	0862-82273
Status	Allied Distillers Ltd
Production status	Operational
Reception Centre	No
Established	1790
Source	Struie Hill
Age when bottled	5, 10 years
Strength	40%

TASTING NOTES	(10 year old)
Nose	Pronounced and distinctive fragrance of smoke and sweetness.
Taste	Good lingering flavour, long-lasting with a slender hint of sweetness.
Comments	A fine dram anytime. Bottled by Ballantines.

PERSONAL NOTES

Brand	**CLYNELISH** (*Kline-leesh*)
Distillery	Clynelish BRORA Sutherland KW9 6LR
Status	United Distillers
Production status	Operational
Reception Centre	Yes. Tel: 0408-621444. Open all year. Mon-Fri: 09.30-16.30
Established	1967-8
Source	Clynmilton Burn
Age when bottled	14 years
Strength	43%

TASTING NOTES

Nose	Quite peaty for a Northern malt.
Taste	Rich, pleasant with a slightly dry finish — lots of character.
Comments	Good after-dinner malt. Popular amongst the connoisseurs.

PERSONAL NOTES

Brand	**DALMORE**
Distillery	Dalmore ALNESS Ross-shire
Telephone	0349-882362
Status	Whyte & Mackay Distillers Ltd
Production status	Operational
Reception Centre	No
Established	c1839
Source	River Alness
Age when bottled	12 years
Strength	40%, 43% for export

TASTING NOTES

Nose	Rich, fresh, with a suggestion of sweetness.
Taste	Full flavour which finishes a touch dry.
Comments	Another really good malt. After-dinner.

PERSONAL NOTES

Brand	# DALWHINNIE
Distillery	Dalwhinnie DALWHINNIE Inverness-shire
Status	United Distillers UK
Production status	Operational
Reception Centre	Tel: 05282-208. Mon-Fri 09.30-17.00 Open all year.
Established	1897-8
Source	Allt an t'Sluic Burn
Age when bottled	15 years
Strength	43%

TASTING NOTES

Nose	A gentle aromatic bouquet.
Taste	A luscious flavour with a light honey sweet finish.
Comments	Pre-dinner, and part of United Distillers' Classic Malt range.

PERSONAL NOTES

Malt	**GLEN ALBYN**
Distillery	Glen Albyn INVERNESS Inverness-shire (Dismantled 1986)
Established	c1846

TASTING NOTES	*(20 year old, 46%)*
Nose	Light and smoky. Pleasant.
Taste	Well-rounded, smoky with a full finish.
Comments	Obviously a depreciating asset, so buy some while stocks last! See page 139.

PERSONAL NOTES

20 yo CAIRNWHIAL

Malt	**GLEN MHOR**
Distillery	Glen Mhor
	INVERNESS
	Inverness-shire
	(Dismantled 1986)
Established	1892
TASTING NOTES	*(8 year old, 40%)*
Nose	Light, sweet fragrance.
Taste	Light-bodied with a slightly dry finish.
Comments	Good, all-round drinking which again will soon be lost for good. See page 139.

PERSONAL NOTES

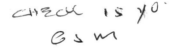

Brand	**GLENMORANGIE**
Distillery	Glenmorangie TAIN Ross-shire IV19 1PZ
Telephone	0862-892043
Status	Macdonald Martin Distilleries plc
Production status	Operational
Reception Centre	No, but visitors are welcome. Phone in advance.
Established	1843
Source	Tarlogie Springs
Age when bottled	10, 18 years old
Strength	40%, 43% and cask strength
TASTING NOTES	*(10 year old, 40%)*
Nose	Beautiful aroma. Fresh and sweet with a subtle hint of peat.
Taste	Medium-bodied with a sweet, fresh finish. One to linger and dwell upon.
Comments	An excellent malt, very popular. Now available at cask strength too. Entire distillery output is sold as single bottled malt.

PERSONAL NOTES

Brand	**GLEN ORD**
Distillery	Ord MUIR of ORD Ross-shire IV6 7UJ
Status	United Distillers
Production status	Operational
Reception Centre	Mon-Fri: 09.30-17.00. Tel: 0463-870421
Established	1838
Source	Lochs Nan Eun and Nam Bonnach
Age when bottled	12 years
Strength	40%

TASTING NOTES

Nose	A beautifully deep nose, with a tinge of dryness.
Taste	Good depth with a long-lasting, delicious aftertaste. Very smooth.
Comments	After-dinner and none too easy to find.

PERSONAL NOTES

Malt	**MILLBURN**
Distillery	Millburn INVERNESS Inverness-shire (Dismantled 1988)
Established	c1807
TASTING NOTES	*(13 year old, 46%)*
Nose	A rich aroma with a faint sweetness.
Taste	Full-bodied, a touch of fruit and a good long finish.
Comments	Sadly, the last distillery to close in Inverness. Still available, see page 140.

PERSONAL NOTES

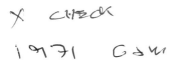

X check

1971   G&M

Malt	# PULTENEY *(Pult-nay)*
Distillery	Pulteney Huddart Street WICK Caithness KW1 5BA
Telephone	0955-2371
Status	Allied Distillers Ltd
Production status	Operational
Reception Centre	No
Established	1826
Source	Loch of Hempriggs
TASTING NOTES	*(8 year old, 40%)*
Nose	Fine, delicate, light aroma with a hint of the Island malts.
Taste	Light, crisp and refreshing with a hint of fullness which gives a positive finish of length.
Comments	An excellent aperitif whisky. The most northerly mainland distillery. See page 140, also available as *Old Pulteney*.

PERSONAL NOTES

Brand	**ROYAL BRACKLA**
Distillery	Royal Brackla NAIRN Morayshire
Status	United Distillers
Production status	Operational
Reception Centre	No
Established	c1812
Source	The Cawdor Burn
Age when bottled	10 years
Strength	43%

TASTING NOTES

Nose	A complex balance of peat and smoke with a touch of sweetness.
Taste	Big, and the peaty-smoky nose comes through on the palate with a hint of fruit and a dry finish.
Comments	Enjoying full production again.

PERSONAL NOTES

Malt	**TEANINICH**
Distillery	Teaninich
	ALNESS
	Ross-shire
Status	United Distillers
Production status	Operational
Reception Centre	No
Established	1817
Source	The Dairywell Spring
TASTING NOTES	*(26 year old, 46%)*
Nose	Subtle, fruity with a gentle bouquet.
Taste	Soft, full of flavour and a delight to drink. Really warms the palate.
Comments	An excellent pre-dinner malt. See Page 140.

PERSONAL NOTES

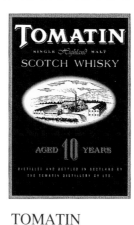

Brand	**TOMATIN**
Distillery	Tomatin TOMATIN Inverness-shire IV13 7YT
Status	Subsidiary of Takara Shuzo & Okura & Co Ltd
Production status	Operational
Reception Centre	Tel: 08082-234. Easter to October from 09.30-16.30. Guided tours, Mon-Thu: 09.30-12.00, 14.00-15.30. Fri: 09.30-12.00, 14.00 only. Tastings.
Established	1897
Source	Allt na Frithe Burn
Age when bottled	10 years old, 10 & 12 for export
Strength	40% and both 40 & 43% for export
Special bottlings	Limited edition — 25 year old

TASTING NOTES

Nose	Pleasant and light.
Taste	Light body, very smooth.
Comments	A pre-dinner dram and a good introduction to malt whisky. The distillery was the first to be acquired by the Japanese in 1985.

PERSONAL NOTES

THE EASTERN HIGHLANDS

Malt	**BANFF**
Distillery	Banff
	BANFF
	Banffshire
Status	Defunct
Established	1863

TASTING NOTES	*(1974, 40%)*
Nose	Very light with a trace of smoke.
Taste	Slightly aggressive, finishing a touch fiery. Nonetheless a good bite.
Comments	A rare dram. The distillery is not listed by the owners United Distillers. See page 138.

PERSONAL NOTES

X CHzer

1974   Gsvu

Malt	# GLENCADAM
Distillery	Glencadam BRECHIN Angus DD9 7PA
Status	Allied Distillers Ltd
Production status	Operational
Reception Centre	Tel: 03562-2217. Mon-Thu, afternoon tours
Established	c1825
Source	Springs in the Unthank Hills

TASTING NOTES	*(1974, 40%)*
Nose	Light hint of sweetness.
Taste	Full, with quite a fruity flavour and a good finish.
Comments	An after-dinner malt. See page 139.

PERSONAL NOTES

Brand	**GLEN DEVERON**
Distillery	Macduff
	BANFF
	Banffshire AB4 3JT
Telephone	0261-812612
Status	General Beverage Corporation, Luxembourg
Production status	Operational
Reception Centre	No
Established	1962-3
Source	Local spring
Age when bottled	12 years, as well as 5 for export
Strength	40%. Export: 12 y.o — 40% & 43%
	5 y.o — 40%

TASTING NOTES

Nose	A pronounced, refreshing bouquet.
Taste	Medium weight and a smooth, pleasant flavour and a clean finish.
Comments	After-dinner dram. Also available as *MacDuff* from the independent bottlers. See page 140.

PERSONAL NOTES

GLENESK

YEARS **12** OLD
SINGLE MALT
HIGHLAND SCOTCH WHISKY

Wm Sanderson Son, Ltd.
Distillers, South Queensferry, Scotland
Bottled in Scotland
40% vol   75 cl

Brand	**GLEN ESK**
Distillery	Glen Esk
	Hillside
	MONTROSE
	Angus
Status	United Distillers
Production status	Mothballed
Reception Centre	No
Established	1897
Source	River North Esk
Age when bottled	12 years
Strength	40%

TASTING NOTES

Nose	A light, delicate hint of sweetness.
Taste	Quite full and sweet with a lingering finish, well balanced.
Comments	After-dinner. The distillery was once known as North Esk and also as Hillside, but the whisky is almost unobtainable.

PERSONAL NOTES

Brand	**GLEN GARIOCH**
	(*Glengeerie*)
Distillery	Glen Garioch
	OLDMELDRUM
	Aberdeenshire AB5 0ES
Telephone	06512-2706
Status	Morrison Bowmore Distillers Ltd
Production status	Operational
Reception Centre	No
Maltings	Floor maltings
Established	1798
Source	Springs on Percock Hill
Age when bottled	8 & 21 years
Strength	43%

TASTING NOTES	(*21 year old*)
Nose	Delicate and smoky.
Taste	Pronounced, peaty flavour with a smooth, pleasant finish.
Comments	Good after-dinner dram, from a distillery which utilises waste heat to cultivate tomatoes and pot-plants!

PERSONAL NOTES

Malt	**GLENUGIE**
Distillery	Glenugie PETERHEAD Aberdeenshire (no longer licensed)
Established	c1831
TASTING NOTES	(20 year old, 46%)
Nose	Hint of ripe fruit.
Taste	Initial trace of sweetness, firm, malty but with a quick, dry finish.
Comments	Pre-dinner and becoming increasingly rare. See page 139.

PERSONAL NOTES

X CHeck

1966 Gavin

CLOSED

Brand	**GLENURY-ROYAL**
Distillery	Glenury-Royal STONEHAVEN Kincardineshire
Status	United Distillers
Production status	Closed
Reception Centre	No
Established	c1825
Source	Cowie Water
Age when bottled	12 years
Strength	40%

TASTING NOTES

Nose	A light hint of smoke with a dry aroma.
Taste	Light body with a dry, smoky finish.
Comments	A good introductory malt, suitable for pre-dinner drinking.

PERSONAL NOTES

Malt	**NORTH PORT**
Distillery	North Port BRECHIN Angus
Status	United Distillers
Production status	Closed
Reception Centre	No
Established	c1820
Source	Loch Lee
TASTING NOTES	(1970 40%)
Nose	A rather sharp, pronounced aroma, almost like a pickle.
Taste	Starts sweet, but quickly fades to spirit — quite a sharp tang.
Comments	Pre-dinner, and preferably with water. See page 140.

PERSONAL NOTES

X CHECK

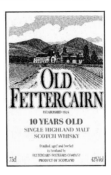

Brand	**OLD FETTERCAIRN**
Distillery	Fettercairn LAURENCEKIRK Kincardineshire
Telephone	05614-244
Status	Whyte & Mackay Distillers Ltd
Production status	Operational
Reception Centre	Tel: 05614-205. Open May to Sept Mon-Sat: 10.00-16.30 (Last tour at 16.00)
Established	c1824
Source	Springs in the Grampian Mountains
Age when bottled	10 years
Strength	40%, 43% for export

TASTING NOTES

Nose	Light, stimulating fresh aroma.
Taste	Fresh, slightly dry finish which is quite stimulating but gently restrained.
Comments	A good all-round drink. Reputed to be the second distillery licensed after the legislation of 1823.

PERSONAL NOTES

Brand	**ROYAL LOCHNAGAR**
Distillery	Lochnagar Crathie BALLATER Aberdeenshire AB3 5TB
Status	United Distillers
Production status	Operational
Reception Centre	Yes, one of the best. Tel: 03397-42273 Open every day 10.00-17.00. In winter, Sunday 11.00-16.00.
Established	1826
Source	Local springs below Lochnagar
Age when bottled	12 years and no age given
Strength	40% and 43%
TASTING NOTES	*(12 year old, 40%)*
Nose	Pleasant, full nose.
Taste	Good body with a full, malt-fruit-like taste and a delicious trace of sweetness.
Comments	Royal Lochnagar Selected Reserve is a special bottling available from time to time at 43%. Expect to pay around £100!

PERSONAL NOTES

THE SOUTHERN HIGHLANDS

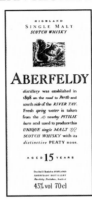

Brand	**ABERFELDY**
Distillery	Aberfeldy ABERFELDY Perthshire PH5 2EB
Status	United Distillers
Production status	Operational
Reception Centre	Yes. Tel: 0887-20330. Mon-Fri: 09.30-16.30, Easter to October. Restricted in Winter
Established	1896
Source	Pitilie Burn
Age when bottled	15 years
Strength	43%
TASTING NOTES	*(1969 distillation)*
Nose	Fresh clean with a lightly peated nose.
Taste	Substantial flavour with a good round taste.
Comments	Now readily available.

PERSONAL NOTES

Brand	# BLAIR ATHOL
Distillery	Blair Athol PITLOCHRY Perthshire PH16 5LY
Status	United Distillers
Production status	Operational
Reception Centre	Tel: 0796-2234. Open all year, Mon-Sat: 09.30-17.00. Easter to October, Sun: 12.00-17.30
Established	1798
Source	Kinnaird Burn
Age when bottled	12 years
Strength	43%

TASTING NOTES

Nose	Light, fresh, clean aroma.
Taste	Medium hint of peat with a round finish. Plenty of flavour.
Comments	Pre-dinner and a distillery well worth visiting.

PERSONAL NOTES

Brand	**DEANSTON**
Distillery	Deanston DOUNE Perthshire FK16 6AR
Telephone	0786-841422
Status	Burn Stewart Distillers plc
Production status	Operational
Reception Centre	No
Established	1965-6, from the cotton mill established on same site c1785
Source	River Teith
Age when bottled	12 years, 17 & 21 for export
Strength	40%

TASTING NOTES

Nose	A hint of sweetness.
Taste	Light, finishing with a smooth trace of the same.
Comments	A pre-dinner malt from a distillery where the vaulted weaving sheds now act as bonds and where a small hydro-electric station has been running for the past three years.

PERSONAL NOTES

Brand	**EDRADOUR** *(Edra-dower)*
Distillery	Edradour PITLOCHRY Perthshire PH16 5JP
Status	Campbell Distillers Ltd
Production status	Operational
Reception Centre	Tel: 0796-472095. Mar-Oct: 09.30-17.00. Nov-Feb, Mon-Sat: 10.30-16.00. Tour, tasting, shop, audio visual
Established	c1837
Maltings	Yes, but currently redundant
Source	Local springs on Mhoulin Moor
Age when bottled	10 years
Strength	40%, 43% for export
TASTING NOTES	*(18 year old, 46%)*
Nose	Fruity-sweet and smoky.
Taste	Strong marzipan taste which comes through smooth, slightly dry and malty with a nutty almond-like aftertaste.
Comments	Scotland's smallest distillery and therefore closest to a working 19th century distillery. Well worth a visit to see how it used to be done.

PERSONAL NOTES

Brand	**GLENGOYNE**
Distillery	Glengoyne DUMGOYNE Stirlingshire G63 9LB
Status	Lang Brothers Ltd
Production status	Operational
Reception Centre	Tel: 0360-50254
Established	c1833
Source	Distillery Burn from Campsie Hills
Age when bottled	10, 12 & 17 years
Strength	10 year old - 40%; 17 year old — 43% Export: 12 year old — 40 & 43% 17 year old — 43%
Special bottlings	Vintage bottlings distilled on Christmas Day, 1967

TASTING NOTES	*(10 year old)*
Nose	A light, fresh aroma.
Taste	Light, pleasant all-round malt.
Comments	Another great introduction to malts. The 17 year old is impressive. Only unpeated malt is used at Glengoyne. There are only 2500 bottles of the vintage available!

PERSONAL NOTES

Brand	**THE GLENTURRET**
Distillery	Glenturret CRIEFF Perthshire PH7 4HA
Status	The Highland Distilleries Co plc
Production status	Operational
Reception Centre	Tel: 0764-2424. Heritage Centre with Water of Life & Spirit of the Glen Exhibition. Tasting bar, Smuggler's Restaurant & Pagoda Room. Mar-Dec, Mon-Sat: 09.30-06.30. Jan-Feb, Mon-Fri: 11.30-04.30
Established	1775
Source	Loch Turret
Age when bottled	8, 12, 15 years
Strength	40%
Special bottlings	1967 @ 50%, 1966 24 y.o @ 40%, 15 y.o @ 50%, 25 y.o Decanter @ 40%, 21 y.o Flagon @ 40%

TASTING NOTES	*(12 year old)*
Nose	Very impressive aromatic nose.
Taste	Full, lush body with a good depth of flavour and a stimulating finish. Delightful.
Comments	Has won three consecutive international gold medals. Arguably Scotland's oldest distillery.

PERSONAL NOTES

Brand	**INCHMURRIN**
Distillery	Loch Lomond ALEXANDRIA Dunbartonshire
Status	Glen Catrine Bonded Warehouse Ltd
Production status	Operational
Reception Centre	No
Established	1965-6
Source	Loch Lomond
Age when bottled	None given and 12 years
Strength	40%

TASTING NOTES

Nose	Slightly aromatic. Follows through on the palate.
Taste	Light bodied. Most of the flavour is on the front of the palate and thus finishes quickly.
Comments	A good everyday drinking malt. Predinner. Formerly owned by ADP and then Inver House Distillers, the distillery is capable of producing two malts from stills similar to those at Littlemill. Two new stills have just been installed.

PERSONAL NOTES

Brand	**TULLIBARDINE**
	(*Tully-bardeen*)
Distillery	Tullibardine
	BLACKFORD
	Perthshire PH4 1QG
Telephone	0764-82252
Status	The Invergordon Distillers Group Plc
Production status	Operational
Reception Centre	By appointment only
Established	1949
Source	The Danny Burn
Age when bottled	10 years
Strength	40%, 43% for export.
Special bottlings	Stillman's Dram occasionally available. Current stocks are 25 y.o.

TASTING NOTES

Nose	Delicate, mellow, sweet aroma of fruit.
Taste	Full-bodied, with a fruity flavour and a good lingering taste.
Comments	A pre-dinner dram from another distillery designed by W Delmé-Evans.

PERSONAL NOTES

THE WESTERN HIGHLANDS

Brand	**BEN NEVIS**
Distillery	Ben Nevis FORT WILLIAM Inverness-shire PH33 6TJ
Telephone	0397-702476
Status	Ben Nevis Distillery Ltd
Production status	Operational
Reception Centre	Tel: 0397-700200. Jan-Oct: 09.00-17.00 Guided tour, audio visual, shop and snack bar
Established	c1825
Source	Allt a Mhullin on Ben Nevis
Age when bottled	4, 12 & 21 years old
Strength	4 & 12 y.o @ 40%, 21 y.o @ 43% Export @ 43%
Special bottlings	19 & 25 y.o bottled at cask strength
TASTING NOTES	*(24 year old, 46%)*
Nose	Full aroma of ripe fruit and sweetness.
Taste	Big, round and smooth with a dominating sweetness which suddenly fades away.
Comments	Rather a tantalising experience of fruit and spirit, almost a liqueur. Distillery is owned by Nikka Distillers of Japan.

PERSONAL NOTES

Malt	**GLENLOCHY**
Distillery	Glenlochy FORT WILLIAM Inverness-shire
Status	United Distillers
Production status	Closed
Reception Centre	No
Maltings	Only the buildings
Established	1898
Source	River Nevis
TASTING NOTES	*(26 year old, 46%)*
Nose	Light and aromatic.
Taste	Light, spicy flavour which tends to finish quickly.
Comments	Pre-dinner drinking and no longer produced. See page 139.

PERSONAL NOTES

OBAN
Little Bay of Caves

OBAN DISTILLERY

SINGLE
MALT

WEST HIGHLAND MALT
SCOTCH WHISKY

43% vol   75 cl ℮

Brand	**OBAN**
Distillery	Oban
	Stafford Street
	OBAN
	Argyll PA34 5NH
Status	United Distillers
Production status	Operational
Reception Centre	Tel: 0631-62110. Open all year. Mon-Fri: 09.30-17.00 also Saturday from Easter to October. Shop, exhibition and tours. Last tour starts at 16.15.
Established	c1794
Source	Loch Gleann a Bhearraidh
Age when bottled	14 years
Strength	43%

TASTING NOTES

Nose	Fresh hint of peat.
Taste	Firm, malty flavour finishing very smoothly. Quite silky.
Comments	One of United Distillers' Classic Malt range. An excellent anytime dram from a distillery founded by the Stevensons.

PERSONAL NOTES

THE LOWLANDS

The modern difference between Lowland malt and that originating from the other regions is simply one of style. Historically, the distinguishing factors were more numerous. In the late 18th century the product of the discreet Highland still (be it legal or illegal) was considered a wholesome, hand-crafted product which was in great demand in the urban markets, but the larger Lowland distillers produced a relatively coarse whisky (rarely made purely from malted barley alone) in huge industrial stills in an effort to supply both the city drinkers and the lucrative London market. This distinction was created by the industrial Lowland distillers who aggressively exploited whatever Government legislation was in force. The distinctions were magnified by the drawing of the 'Highland Line' which effectively stretched from Greenock on the Clyde to Dundee on the Tay and split the country into two regions gauged by two separate sets of Excise regulations due to the disparity between their respective products.

Eventually the technical differences were removed when more realistic early-19th century Government Acts encouraged illicit distillers in the Highlands to go legal and allowed all producers to distil on a more equal basis. The massive grain distilleries of the central belt may be fewer now but they are still the sole remaining throwback to the days when the Steins and the Haigs wielded some of the most powerful industrial might in Scotland.

Although there is now a relatively low amount of distilling in the Lowlands, small malt distilleries were once in abundance even in the late 19th century. In the remote south west corner, over a dozen concerns existed stretching from Stranraer to Annan. Only Bladnoch Distillery survives and although the substantial remains of two distilleries at Langholm and Annan can still be viewed the malt they once produced has long been drunk away.

Fortunately we can still sample many good malts

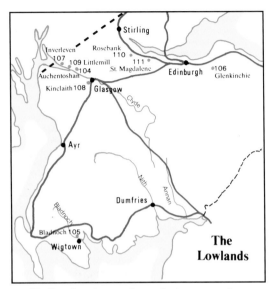

Distillery location numbers refer to page numbers

in the Lowland region. Scotland's most southerly is produced at Bladnoch, a beautifully located distillery with a reception centre which is well worth the drive from Dumfries along the famous Solway coast. Just up the road from Bladnoch, at Girvan on the Ayrshire coast the less famous Ladyburn malt has now ceased to be produced beside Wm Grant's grain whisky distillery. It cannot even be obtained from the independent bottlers.

But most of the Lowland malts are produced to the north along the Highland line. In the Glasgow area, just north of the Clyde along the A82 route to Loch Lomond lies Auchentoshan Distillery, which is one of the two Lowland distilleries still employing the technique of triple-distillation. This distillery has catered well for the visitor in the past with one of the first reception centres to be established in Scotland but this facility is unfortunately closed at present. Littlemill Distillery at Bowling lies nearby, and employed triple distillation until the 1930's. Kinclaith malt still exists although the distillery is now no longer in existence having once been part of Long John's Strathclyde grain distilling complex. Another malt in a similar position is Inverleven which emanates from the curious Lomond stills at the malt distillery within Hiram Walker's vast grain distillery at Dumbarton. Rosebank, which lies nearer Edinburgh at Falkirk, is similar to Auchentoshan in that it too employs triple distillation and the result is one of the great Lowland malts, highly regarded as a pre-dinner dram and a wonderful surprise to anyone drinking their first malt whisky. Not far away at Linlithgow, St Magdalene is now defunct but the malt is still available from the independent bottlers.

Much of Edinburgh's prosperity has been built on brewing and distilling although the industry is greatly reduced within the city now. There are no malt distilleries operating now and all activity is concentrated in producing grain whisky. However, to the east of the city Glenkinchie Distillery at Pencaitland was one of the first to cater for visitors. It also has an interesting collection of museum pieces and gives a thorough insight into the 'tools of the trade'. This malt is bottled as a brand under the Classic Malt banner by United Distillers, but all of them are worth looking out for and give a good indication of the Lowland style — light, fragrant and an excellent way to start drinking malt whisky.

Brand	**AUCHENTOSHAN**
Distillery	Auchentoshan DALMUIR Dunbartonshire
Telephone	0389-78561
Status	Morrison Bowmore Distillers Ltd
Production status	Operational
Reception Centre	No
Established	c1800
Source	Kilpatrick Hills
Age when bottled	10 & 21 years
Strength	10 y.o — 40%; 21 y.o — 43% Export — 43%

TASTING NOTES	(10 year old)
Nose	Delicate, slightly sweet.
Taste	Light, soft sweetness with a good aftertaste.
Comments	A triple-distilled malt from one of Scotland's most accessible distilleries. Popular and readily available at home and abroad.

PERSONAL NOTES

Brand	**BLADNOCH**
Distillery	Bladnoch BLADNOCH Wigtownshire DG8 9AB
Status	United Distillers
Production status	Operational
Reception Centre	Yes. A charming place to visit. Mon-Fri:10.00-16.00. Tel: 09884-2235.
Established	1817
Source	Loch Ma Berry
Age when bottled	10 years
Strength	43%

TASTING NOTES

Nose	Very light and delicate.
Taste	Smooth, delicate but full and easy to drink.
Comments	Scotland's most southerly distillery. A pre-dinner malt which is now highly regarded — particularly the rare vintages.

PERSONAL NOTES

Brand	# GLENKINCHIE
Distillery	Glenkinchie PENTCAITLAND East Lothian EH34 5ET
Telephone	0875-340451
Status	United Distillers
Production status	Operational
Reception Centre	Yes. Mon-Fri: 09.30-16.00 Classic Malts video, tour, bowling green, shop.
Established	c1837
Source	Lammermuir Hills
Age when bottled	10 years
Strength	43%

TASTING NOTES

Nose	Light fragrant sweetness.
Taste	Round flavour, slightly dry with a lingering smoothness.
Comments	An excellent pre-dinner dram, now available as part of United Distillers' Classic Malt range.

PERSONAL NOTES

Malt	# INVERLEVEN
Distillery	Inverleven DUMBARTON Strathclyde
Status	Allied Distillers Ltd
Reception centre	No
Established	1938
Source	Loch Lomond

TASTING NOTES	*(17 year old, 46%)*
Nose	Delicate hint of smoke.
Taste	Quite full-bodied. Smooth with a round palate.
Comments	Rarely available unless obtained from one of the independent bottlers. See page 140.

PERSONAL NOTES

Malt	**KINCLAITH**
Distillery	Kinclaith, Moffat Street GLASGOW
Status	Last licensed to Long John Distillers
Production status	Defunct. Dismantled 1975
Established	1957-8
TASTING NOTES	*(18 year old, 46%)*
Nose	Light and smoky with a spirit sharpness.
Taste	Full-bodied, smooth with an attractive finish.
Comments	No longer with us and now in very limited supply. You are unlikely to find this on the high street. See page 140

PERSONAL NOTES

X CHECK

1967 G & M

Brand	**LITTLEMILL**
Distillery	Littlemill BOWLING Dunbartonshire G60 5BG
Telephone	0389-74154
Status	Gibson International Ltd
Production status	Operational
Reception Centre	Limited tours by prior arrangement. 08.30-16.00
Established	1772
Source	Kilpatrick Hills
Age when bottled	8 years
Strength	Home trade — 40% Export — 40% & 43%

TASTING NOTES

Nose	Light and delicate.
Taste	Mellow-flavoured, light, slightly cloying yet pleasant and warming.
Comments	Pre-dinner, from a distillery full of interesting, novel features. Certainly one of the oldest in Scotland.

PERSONAL NOTES

Brand	**ROSEBANK**
Distillery	Rosebank
	Camelon
	FALKIRK
	Stirlingshire
Status	United Distillers
Production status	Operational
Reception Centre	No. Visiting by appointment. Tel: 0324-23325.
Established	c1840
Source	Carron Valley reservoir
Age when bottled	12 years
Strength	43%

TASTING NOTES

Nose	Light, yet delicate.
Taste	Well balanced, good flavour with entirely acceptable astringency.
Comments	A triple-distilled malt suitable for pre-dinner drinking.

PERSONAL NOTES

Malt	**ST MAGDALENE**
Distillery	St Magdalene LINLITHGOW West Lothian
Status	United Distillers
Production status	Defunct
Reception centre	No
Maltings	Converted into accommodation
Established	c1798
Source	Loch Lomond
TASTING NOTES	*(20 year old, 46%)*
Nose	A round aroma with a touch of smoke.
Taste	Full-bodied, smooth with a ripe finish and much character.
Comments	After-dinner malt. See page 140.

PERSONAL NOTES

X CHECK

25 Y O

CAIDENHEAD

ISLAY

O f all Scotland's malts, the Islays are perhaps the most easily recognised. But even so, there are some surprises within this group which are traditionally held to be amongst the heaviest and most pungent available. Their most recognisable characteristics are due to production methods which were developed in concert with the available distilling ingredients in this remote locality. While the mainland markets were supplied by mainland distillers in the 18th and 19th centuries, the islanders supplied a local market from stills — both legal and illegal — which were operated from farmyards, bothies on the bleak moors above Port Ellen and remote caves along the precipitous coast of the Oa.

Islay, renowned as the most fertile island in the Hebrides, had three major assets in this development, a ready source of local barley — or bere as it was then known — inexhaustible amounts of peat and burns running brim-full of soft water. Coupled to this was the likelihood that the art of distilling was probably brought to Scotland via Islay by the Irish in the 15th century. It is impossible to visit Islay and not notice the peat. Along the roadside crossing the enormous Laggan Bog between Port Ellen and Bowmore the peat banks spread as far as the eye can see. This fuel was the only means by which the islanders could dry their grain which was an essential process not only for distilling but also for storage during the wet seasons. By kilning barley it could be kept longer and the dryer the grain was, the less likely it was to go mouldy.

As the grain dried in the fumes, the peat imparted to the barley a highly distinctive character which manifested itself when the spirit was finally distilled from it. These characteristics are still apparent in today's Islay malts and are best experienced by trying Ardbeg, Lagavulin and Laphroaig which form the three most traditional Islay malts.

The other Islays display this peaty-smoky

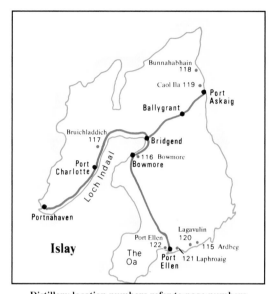

Distillery location numbers refer to page numbers

characteristic to a lesser degree but it is always detectable nonetheless.

It is good to see that the Islay distillers, despite their more remote location, are always able to accommodate visitors and some of the distilleries are spectacularly situated. All of them have one thing in common — they are built on the seashore. A century ago this afforded them the access to the sea and thus the mainland markets. The smaller inland farmyard distilleries had by then been unable to compete and one by one they closed down. But it is still possible to see the sites of these traditional distilleries, most notably at Octomore Farm behind Port Charlotte, at Tallant Farm above Bowmore and at Lossit Kennels by Bridgend. Of the present distilleries perhaps Bowmore is most favourably endowed for the visitor. Not only does it produce a memorable dram but is has a superb reception centre and donated one of its bonded warehouses to the Islay and Jura community who, with a quite magnificent effort, raised enough money to build a swimming pool within it. In the south of the island Lagavulin and Laphroaig both cater well for the visitor and are magnificently located by the sea. Ardbeg — now producing again — is a more sobering prospect given that the distillery was once the centre of a large community. Port Ellen is still closed but the associated maltings are at last being put to better use and are supplying not only Lagavulin and Caol Ila with malt, but also some of the other non-UD distilleries on the island.

Across Loch Indaal from Bowmore lies Bruichladdich which, like Bunnahabhain, produces one of the lighter Islays. This distillery was one of the first in the Hebrides to be constructed from concrete in 1881. Near Port Askaig, at the point where you cross to Jura, lie Caol Ila and Bunnahabhain with spectacular views of the Paps of Jura. Caol Ila is as modern and efficient a distillery as you are likely to find and the stillhouse alone is worth seeing. The dram is now readily available and it is a good Islay, as is its close neighbour which was built in 1880-1.

Bunnahabhain is for many people the best introduction to the Islays since it is neither too heavy nor too light, and for many newcomers to the Islays it remains their favourite dram. A trip around Scotland's malts cannot be considered complete unless the Islays are undertaken with fervour for it is in their makeup that the blender finds his greatest inspiration, the enthusiast finds his greatest experience and the taster finds his greatest joy.

Brand	**ARDBEG**
Distillery	Ardbeg
	PORT ELLEN
	Islay
	Argyll
Telephone	0496-2244
Status	Allied Distillers Ltd
Production status	Operational
Reception Centre	No
Established	c1794
Source	Lochs Arinambeast and Uigedale
Age when bottled	10 years
Strength	40%

TASTING NOTES

Nose	Lovely peaty aroma with a hint of sweetness.
Taste	Full-bodied and luscious with an excellent aftertaste.
Comments	Good after-dinner malt. Perhaps the ultimate test for beginners?

PERSONAL NOTES

Brand	**BOWMORE**
Distillery	Bowmore
	BOWMORE
	Islay
	Argyll
Telephone	049681-441
Status	Morrison Bowmore Distillers Ltd
Production status	Operational
Reception Centre	Yes, the best in the islands. Tel: 049681-671. Shop, tastings, audio-visual. From 10.00 weekdays with last tour at 15.30.
Maltings	Floor maltings
Established	c1770
Source	River Laggan
Age when bottled	10, 12, 17, 21, 1969 & 25 years
Strength	40% & 43%, 43% for export

TASTING NOTES

Nose	Light, peaty-smoky.
Taste	Healthy, middle-range Islay with medium weight and a smooth finish.
Comments	One of the best sherrying malts available — the older vintages are outstanding. The swimming pool in one of the bonds makes Bowmore a unique experience!

PERSONAL NOTES

Brand	**BRUICHLADDICH** *(Broo-ich-laddie)*
Distillery	Bruichladdich BRUICHLADDICH Islay, Argyll
Telephone	0496-85221
Status	The Invergordon Distillers Ltd
Production status	Operational
Reception Centre	No. Visitors by appointment.
Established	1881
Source	Local hills
Age when bottled	10 years; Export: 10, 15 & 21 y.o.
Strength	40%, 40 & 43% for export
Special bottlings	Stillman's Dram, currently 25 y.o.

TASTING NOTES

Nose	Light to medium with a good hint of smoke.
Taste	Lingering flavour giving the expected fullness of Islay character whilst lacking the heavier tones.
Comments	A good pre-dinner dram, which is an ideal introduction to the Islay style. The 15-year-old is superb.

PERSONAL NOTES

Brand	**BUNNAHABHAIN**
	(Bu-na-ha-venn)
Distillery	Bunnahabhain
	PORT ASKAIG
	Islay
	Argyll PA46 7RP
Telephone	0496-84646
Status	The Highland Distilleries Co plc
Production status	Operational
Reception Centre	No, but visitors are welcome by appointment
Established	1880-1
Source	Local springs
Age when bottled	12 years
Strength	40%, 43% for export

TASTING NOTES

Nose	Pronounced character with a flowery aroma.
Taste	Not reminiscent of the Islay style, but a lovely round flavour nonetheless.
Comments	A popular after-dinner dram especially in France and the United States.

PERSONAL NOTES

ISLAY
SINGLE MALT *SCOTCH WHISKY*

CAOL ILA

distillery, built in 1846 is situated near Port Askaig on the Isle of Islay. Steamers used to call twice a week to collect whisky from this remote site in a cove facing the Isle of Jura. Water supplies for mashing come from Loch nam Ban although the sea provides water for condensing. Unusual for an Islay this single MALT SCOTCH WHISKY has a fresh aroma and a light yet well rounded flavour.

AGED **15** YEARS

Brand	**CAOL ILA** *(Koal-eela)*
Distillery	Caol Ila PORT ASKAIG Islay Argyll PA46 7RL
Telephone	0496-84207
Status	United Distillers
Production status	Operational
Reception Centre	No. Visiting by appointment.
Established	1846
Source	Loch Nam Ban
Age when bottled	15years
Strength	43%

TASTING NOTES	*(1969 distillation)*
Nose	Light, fresh with a trace of peat.
Taste	Not a heavy Islay, but has pleasing weight and a fairly round flavour. Finishes smoothly.
Comments	Popular after-dinner dram which sherries well. Popular in Italy. Distillery is spectacularly situated on the Sound of Islay.

PERSONAL NOTES

Brand	**LAGAVULIN**
	(Lagga-voolin)
Distillery	Lagavulin
	PORT ELLEN
	Islay
	Argyll PA42 7DZ
Telephone	0496-2400
Status	United Distillers
Production status	Operational
Reception Centre	Yes. Visiting by appointment.
Established	1816 with distilling on the site since at least 1784
Source	Solum Lochs
Age when bottled	16 years
Strength	43%

TASTING NOTES

Nose	A typical Islay — heavy, powerful aroma. Unmistakable.
Taste	Quite heavy and very full with a delightful hint of sweetness at this age.
Comments	Part of United Distillers' Classic Malt range. A gentle giant of a dram. One of the best.

PERSONAL NOTES

LAPHROAIG®

SINGLE ISLAY MALT
SCOTCH WHISKY

10
Years Old

The most richly flavoured of
all Scotch whiskies

ESTABLISHED
1815

DISTILLED AND BOTTLED IN SCOTLAND BY
D. JOHNSTON & CO. (LAPHROAIG), LAPHROAIG DISTILLERY, ISLE OF ISLAY.

40% vol   75 cl

Brand	**LAPHROAIG** *(La-froyg)*
Distillery	Laphroaig PORT ELLEN Islay Argyll PA42 7DU
Telephone	0496-2418
Status	Allied Distillers Ltd
Production status	Operational
Reception Centre	No, but visitors are welcome. Telephone in advance.
Maltings	Floor maltings
Established	1826
Source	Drawn from local mosses
Age when bottled	10 and 15 years
Strength	40%, 43% for export.
TASTING NOTES	*(10 year old)*
Nose	Well balanced, peaty-smoky.
Taste	Full of character, big Islay peaty flavour with a delightful touch of sweetness. Betrays its proximity to the sea.
Comments	An excellent after dinner malt from a beautifully situated distillery. Very popular.

PERSONAL NOTES

Malt	**PORT ELLEN**
Distillery	Port Ellen
	PORT ELLEN, Islay, Argyll
Status	United Distillers
Production status	Mothballed
Reception Centre	No
Maltings	The associated industrial maltings now supply a great deal of the island's malting requirement.
Established	1825
Source	Leorin Lochs

TASTING NOTES	*(1969 distillation)*
Nose	A hint of peat with a delicate bouquet.
Taste	Light for an Islay lacking that characteristic peaty flavour. A dry finish.
Comments	A popular pre-dinner dram. Direct exports to the Americas were first pioneered at Port Ellen in the 1840s.

PERSONAL NOTES

CAMPBELTOWN

Dufftown could lay claim to being Scotland's whisky capital but in the middle of the last century there was only one place which had the right to that name — Campbeltown. Situated on the lee shore of the Mull of Kintyre, this town was literally awash with distillate a hundred years ago. When Alfred Barnard compiled his wonderful book — *The Whisky Distilleries of the United Kingdom* in 1886, he found no less than 21 producing distilleries in and around the town!

These were Hazelburn (established 1836), Springbank (1828), Dalintober (1832), Benmore (1868), Ardlussa (1879), Dalaruan (1824), Lochead (1824), Glen Nevis (1877), Kinloch (1823), Burnside (1825), Glengyle (1873), Lochruan (1835), Albyn (1830), Scotia (1832), Rieclachan (1825), Glenside (1830), Longrow (1824), Kintyre (c1826), Campbeltown(1815), Argyll (1844) and Springside (1830).

The number of operations were a throwback to the days when illicit distillation in the district was rife, and was not entirely discouraged by the landowners, or indeed by the law. Barnard relates an apocryphal tale:

> *A capital story is told of an aged woman who resided near Hazelburn. She was of rather doubtful character and was charged before the Sheriff with smuggling. The charge being held proven, it fell to his lordship to pronounce sentence, When about to do so he thus addressed the culprit, 'I dare say my poor woman it is not often you have been found guilty of this fault.' 'Deed no Sheriff', she readily replied, 'I haena made a drap since yaun wee keg I sent to yersel.'*

Campbeltown's boom period was based upon a ready and huge market in cheap Scotch within the working population in the industrial central belt and

Dalintober Distillery

the avaricious desire of the distillers to supply that
market come what may.

A local coal seam seemed perfect as a cheap
source of fuel, but its exhaustion was to prove fatal,
and as the late Victorian boom in whisky distilling
collapsed so too did distilling in Campbeltown. The
sad reminder of the industry's presence in the town is
now manifested in two distilleries, Glen Scotia and
Springbank, which are each producing at present,
although Glen Scotia is sending its distillate to its
sister distillery, Littlemill, near Dumbarton, to
mature.

It would be unwise to forget Campbeltown's
contribution to distilling despite the fact that it is
unlikely more distilleries will ever start up in the
town again. Its product had a unique regional flavour
which came close to the Islay style. This can still be
found in Longrow, a traditional old-fashioned malt
which is distilled at Springbank. Its character differs
from its sister malt Springbank which is a smoother,
more elegant dram — one which has become
phenomenally successful in Japan. That it has
succeeded so well is a tribute to the family which has
always owned the distillery and which has always
recognised its quality.

The drawings which appear here show something

LOCHRUAN DISTILLERY

Lochruan Distillery

of the nature of distilling operations in the 'good old days' in the 1880's. When Barnard visited the town he noted that '... Sunday in Campbeltown is carried to its Jewish length, and is quite a day of gloom and penance... it is said that there are as many places of worship as distilleries in the town'. His remarks, no matter how flippant, are important since they set down a precise record of the 'Golden Age' of distilling in Scotland — a time we are unlikely to experience again. If Campbeltown's decline has served any purpose at all, it will have been to remind us all of the fickle nature of the marketplace.

As a town, Campbeltown is delightfully situated. Its remoteness allows its inhabitants a certain privacy from the mainstream tourist traffic during the summer, but it is always worth considering the detour down the Mull of Kintyre when travelling through this part of the world. The overwhelming impression is that of a thriving fishing and market town, but the names of old distilleries are to be found in a number of nameplaces — Ardlussa, Lochruan, Dalintober and the like. Savour them as you savour a dram in this setting — I have always said that drinking malt at source is the best way to appreciate it. Try it in Campbeltown.

Brand	**GLEN SCOTIA**
Distillery	Glen Scotia High Street CAMPBELTOWN Argyll
Telephone	0586-52288
Status	Gibson International Ltd
Production status	Operational
Reception Centre	Yes, with limited facilities. Open 08.30-16.00
Established	1832
Source	Campbeltown Loch
Age when bottled	8 years
Strength	40%, 43% for export

TASTING NOTES

Nose	Faint touch of smoke. Intense aroma, but still delicate and sweet.
Taste	Light for a Campbeltown. Hint of peat with a good finish.
Comments	Pre-dinner dram. In fact, a good drink at any time.

PERSONAL NOTES

Brand	**LONGROW**
Distillery	Springbank CAMPBELTOWN Argyll PA28 6ET
Telephone	0586-552085
Status	J & A Mitchell & Co Ltd
Production status	Operational
Reception Centre	No
Maltings	Floor maltings
Established	1824
Source	Crosshill Loch
Age when bottled	16 years (1974). Export: 17 y.o.
Strength	46%

TASTING NOTES

Nose	An island-peaty, medicinal aroma.
Taste	Well balanced, with a hint of sweetness. A succulent malty palate and a fine lingering aftertaste. Almost an Islay.
Comments	Distilled at Springbank, but by using entirely peat-dried malted barley, the heavier peated malt results. A dram for the connoisseur.

PERSONAL NOTES

Brand	**SPRINGBANK**
Distillery	Springbank
	CAMPBELTOWN
	Argyll PA28 6ET
Telephone	0586-552085
Status	J & A Mitchell & Co Ltd
Production status	Operational
Reception Centre	No
Maltings	Floor maltings
Established	1828
Source	Crosshill Loch
Age when bottled	15, 21, 25 & 30 years.
Strength	46%
Special bottlings	All 15 y.o. home trade available in Martinique bottles.

TASTING NOTES	*(21 year old, 46%)*
Nose	Positive, rich aroma with a slight sweetness.
Taste	Well balanced, full of charm and elegance. A malt drinker's dream.
Comments	A dependable classic for the malt lover. Superb after-dinner drink — you won't refuse the second one! Bottled at the distillery and now widely available.

PERSONAL NOTES

THE ISLANDS AND N. IRELAND

Recent archaeological finds on the island of Rhum in the Inner Hebrides suggest that the natives knew how to make a brew long before the Irish were credited with introducing the art of distillation to their Scottish cousins. Wm Grant & Son Ltd (makers of Balvenie, Kininvie and Glenfiddich) even went so far as to try and recreate the original 4000 year old recipe which was scientifically reconstructed from scrapings off pottery shards. This brew was drawn from the local herbs, grasses and other vegetation and turned out to be a little immature, but like all good brews it improved with familiarity. The last two centuries may have gradually familiarised the world to Scotch, but we can now lay claim to having played a fundamental part in the history of the development of distillation. And for the present-day visitor to Scotland, the past is manifested in some of the most gloriously situated distilleries in the world.

The styles of these malts differ, partly due to location and partly due to the desires of the distillery operators. For instance Jura, from the island just north of Islay, can be fairly described as a Highland-like dram whereas in the last century it was much closer in style to its Islay neighbours. The reason is that the distillery went out of production in 1901 and was replaced in 1963 with a completely new unit designed by W Delmé-Evans. He had stills of a highland-type design installed and used malt that was only lightly peated. Similarly Tobermory's distillery has had its plant changed over the years and has produced some variable distillations of Ledaig until ceasing production in1980. Happily, it came back on stream in May 1990.

On Skye an altogether more traditional taste is found. Talisker is one of the giants among malt. It is a 'big' whisky in every way with an explosive effect on the palate and a wonderful, peaty, sweetness on the nose. The distillery has changed considerably but still retains some of the more traditional implements

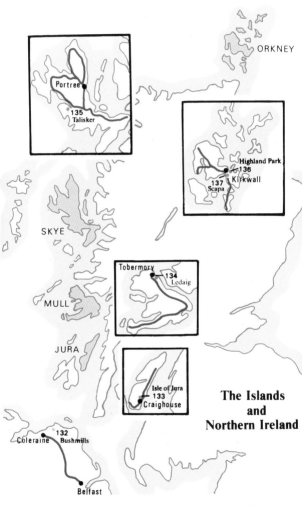

ORKNEY

Portree

135
Talisker

Highland Park
136
Kirkwall
137
Scapa

SKYE

Tobermory
134
Ledaig

MULL

JURA

Isle of Jura
133
Craighouse

**The Islands
and
Northern Ireland**

132
Coleraine Bushmills

Belfast

Distillery location numbers refer to page numbers

associated with 18th and 19th century distilling. For instance, swan-necked lyne arms can be seen dropping into wooden worm tubs outside the stillhouse wall — the same technique illicit distillers used though on a much smaller scale. Talisker's taste is perhaps the most recognisable among the island and western malts and has benefited greatly from the greater exposure it has undoubtedly received from its repackaging and presentation.

Orkney is the most northerly outpost of whisky distilling in Scotland with two very good malts emanating from Highland Park and Scapa. The surrounding Orcadian landscape at first sight appears bleak but its loveliness grows on the visitor just as their malts do. Their style is traditional — they are both very silky in texture and have a very faithful following among enthusiasts.

At the other geographical extreme across the North Channel from Galloway and only 17 miles (27km) from Islay's southern shore lies another island — Ireland. Here, in County Antrim the oldest whiskey distillery in the world (licensed in 1608) is producing a malt whiskey at Bushmills. It would be a nonsense to say it does not have a place in this book given that Islay (and therefore Scotland) probably owes much of its distilling heritage to Ireland. This dram is a pleasant surprise and should not be missed out. Within it I can detect subtle inferences from Islay, Campbeltown and Galloway and as such it should be accepted as part of the family.

Notwithstanding that, the island malts show a tremendous variance in style and texture and are a good way to start an education of what is available to the malt drinker. To anyone who thinks that all malt whisky tastes the same, the island drams are a perfect answer.

Brand	**BUSHMILLS**
Distillery	Bushmills, BUSHMILLS Co. Antrim N. Ireland
Status	Irish Distillers Ltd
Production status	Operational
Reception Centre	Yes. Very popular. Advisable to telephone in advance. Tel: 02657-31521
Established	1608
Source	St Columb's Rill
Age when bottled	10 years
Strength	40%

TASTING NOTES

Nose	Light, smoky, fragrant aroma.
Taste	Reflects the aroma. A very attractive lingering aftertaste of a well matured malt.
Comments	The only Irish malt whiskey from the oldest licensed whiskey distillery in the world. Triple-distilled in the Irish style.

PERSONAL NOTES

Brand	**ISLE OF JURA**
Distillery	Isle of Jura Craighouse JURA Argyll PA60 7XT
Telephone	049682-240
Status	The Invergordon Distillers Group Plc
Reception Centre	No, but visitors are welcome by appointment.
Established	c1810, rebuilt in 1960-3
Source	Market Loch
Age when bottled	10 years
Strength	40%, 40% & 43% for export
Special bottlings	Stillman's Dram, currently 26 y.o.

TASTING NOTES

Nose	Smooth with subtle peaty traces. Dry.
Taste	Well-matured, full but delicate flavour. Good lingering character.
Comments	An almost Highland-like malt created by W Delmé-Evans for drinking anytime. Always worth visiting the distillery by crossing from Port Askaig when you are on Islay.

PERSONAL NOTES

Malt	# LEDAIG
Distillery	Tobermory
	TOBERMORY
	Mull
	Argyll
Status	Tobermory Distillers Ltd
Production status	Operational
Reception Centre	No
Established	1798
Source	Mishnish Lochs

TASTING NOTES	*(No age given, 40%)*
Nose	Fine, fruity nose.
Taste	Gentle flavour with a soft finish. A good, subtle malt.
Comments	Pre-dinner, from a distillery with a fascinating history. More readily available as a vatted malt called Tobermory. See page 140.

PERSONAL NOTES

Brand	**TALISKER**
Distillery	Talisker CARBOST Isle of Skye IV47 8SR
Telephone	047842-203
Status	United Distillers
Production status	Operational
Reception Centre	Yes. Apr-Oct, Mon-Fri: 09.00-16.30. Nov-Mar: by appointment, 14.00- 16.30. Shop, exhibition, distillery tour.
Established	1830-33
Source	Cnoc-nan-Speireag (Hawkhill)
Age when bottled	10 years
Strength	45. 8%

TASTING NOTES

Nose	Heavy sweet and full aroma.
Taste	Unique full flavour which explodes on the palate, lingering with an element of sweetness.
Comments	Superb after-dinner malt from United Distillers' Classic Malt range. One of the best.

PERSONAL NOTES

Brand	**HIGHLAND PARK**
Distillery	Highland Park Holm Road KIRKWALL Orkney KW15 1SU
Telephone	0856-873107
Status	The Highland Distilleries Co plc
Production status	Operational
Reception Centre	Yes. Easter-Oct, Mon-Fri: 10.00-16.00. June-August includes Saturdays. Nov-Easter, Mon-Fri: Tour at 14.30
Maltings	Floor maltings
Established	1795
Source	Cattie Maggie's Spring
Age when bottled	12 years
Strength	40%, 43% in some export countries
Special bottlings	1967 vintage at 43%

TASTING NOTES

Nose	Full of character — pleasant, lingering and smoky.
Taste	Medium, well-balanced flavour finishing with a subtle dryness.
Comments	An excellent after-dinner dram from Scotland's most northerly distillery.

PERSONAL NOTES

Malt	**SCAPA**
Distillery	Scapa ST OLA Orkney KW15 1SE
Telephone	0856-872071
Status	Allied Distillers Ltd
Production status	Operational
Reception Centre	No
Established	1885
Source	Lingro Burn and local springs

TASTING NOTES	*(8 year old, 40%)*
Nose	Delightful aromatic bouquet of peat and heather.
Taste	Medium-bodied with a malty, silk-like finish.
Comments	After-dinner, but only from the independent bottlers. The Navy rescued Scapa from destruction by fire during the First World War! See page 140.

PERSONAL NOTES

INDEPENDENT BOTTLERS

The following malts are available as special bottlings
from the two main Scottish independent bottlers:

Gordon & MacPhail Ltd
50-60 South Street
ELGIN, Morayshire IV30 1JY
Tel: 0343-545111
Gordon and MacPhail usually give the year of distillation
instead of the age when bottled. Strength is normally
40% alcohol by volume.

Cadenheads Whisky Shop
172 Canongate
EDINBURGH EH8 8BN
Tel: 031-556-5864 (retail & mixed cases)
Tel: 0586-52009 (wholesale)
William Cadenhead bottle malts at cask strength and
these are unfiltered. Age varies depending on the cask
being bottled. They still have substantial stock of their
standard bottlings which are normally 46% alcohol by
volume.

The malts listed below are non-commercial brand
bottlings only. Malt whiskies which are not available as
independent bottlings are not listed.

	G&M	Wm Cad
Aberfeldy	1974	
Aberlour		8, 27 y. o.
Allt-a-Bhainne		12 y. o.
Ardbeg	1974	16, 17, 18 y. o.
Ardmore	1977	13 y. o.
Auchroisk		12 y. o.
Balblair	10 y. o. , 1959/64	26 y. o.
Balmenach	1972/73	10, 24 y. o.
Balvenie		12, 15 y. o.
Banff	1974	15 y. o.
Ben Nevis		13 y. o.
Benriach	1976/82	
Benrinnes	1969	17, 18 y. o.
Benromach	1970/71	
Bladnoch	1984	
Blair Athol		23 y. o.
Bowmore		11, 15 y. o.

	G&M	Wm Cad
Braes of Glenlivet		13 y. o.
Bruichladdich	1965	23 y. o.
Caol Ila	1978	13 y. o.
Caperdonich	1968/80/82	14 y. o.
Clynelish	12 y. o.	20 y. o.
Coleburn	1972	13 y. o.
Convalmore	1969	
Cragganmore	1794/76	20 y. o.
Craigellachie	1974	20 y. o.
Dailuaine	1971/72	23, 27 y. o.
Dallas Dhu	10 y. o	
Dalmore		12 y. o.
Dalwhinnie	1970	
Deanston		14 y. o.
Dufftown		12 y. o.
Glen Albyn	1968	17, 26 y. o.
Glenburgie	8 y. o. 1960/66/68	13, 28 y. o.
Glencadam	1974	21, 22, 25 y. o.
Glendronach		22 y. o.
Glenfarclas		11 y. o.
Glenfiddich		12 y. o.
Glen Garioch		16 y. o.
Glenglassaugh		13 y. o.
Glen Grant	15, 21, 25 y. o. 1936/48/49/50/51 52/54/59/60	
Glen Keith	1965	
Glenkinchie	1974	
Glenlivet	12, 15, 21 y. o. 1940/43/46/48 49/50/51/61/63/74	16, 17, 18 y.o.
Glenlochy	1974	
Glenlossie	1972/73	
Glen Mhor	8 y. o. , 1978	15, 17 y. o.
Glenrothes	8 y. o, 1956/57	20 y. o.
Glen Scotia		14 y. o.
Glen Spey		15 y. o.
Glentauchers	1979	13 y. o.
Glenturret		25 y. o.
Glenugie	1966	13 y. o.
Glenury-Royal		23 y. o.
Highland Park	8 y. o. 1959/74/83	12 y. o.
Imperial	1979	
Inchgower		15, 25 y. o.
Inchmurrin		18 y. o.
Inverleven	1979	25 y. o.

	G&M	Wm Cad
Kinclaith	1967	
Knockdhu	1974	
Lagavulin		14 y. o.
Ledaig	1973	
Linkwood	15, 21 y. o. 1939/46/54/61/67	14, 21 y. o.
Littlemill		26 y. o.
Lochside	1966	
Longmorn	12 y. o 1956/62/63/69	12 y. o.
Macallan		11 y. o.
Macduff	1975	14 y. o.
Millburn	1971/72	22 y. o.
Milton Duff		13 y. o.
Mortlach	15, 21 y. o. 1936/38/60/65/66	22 y. o.
Mosstowie	1975	16 y. o
North Port	1970	
Oban	1972	
Old Elgin	8, 15 y. o. 1938/39/40/47/49	
Old Pulteney	15 y. o. , 1961	
Pittyvaich		13 y. o.
Port Ellen	1974/77	10 y. o.
Pulteney		12, 22 y. o.
Rosebank	1979	11 y. o.
Royal Brackla	1972/76	26 y. o.
Scapa	1979	
Speyburn	1971	15 y. o.
St Magdalene	1965	9 y. o.
Strathisla	8, 15, 21, 25 y. o. 1948/49/54/55 58/60/61/74	
Strathmill		12 y. o.
Talisker	1952/55	14 y. o.
Tamdhu	8 y. o. , 1957	14, 29 y. o.
Teaninich	1975/82	27 y. o.
Tomatin	1964/68	13 y. o.
Tomintoul		12, 20 y. o.
Tullibardine		27 y. o.

STOP PRESS

James MacArthur's, 20 Knight's Templar Way, High Wycombe,
Bucks HP11 1PY. Tel: 0494-530740, Fax: 0494-442159
Now supplying vintage 'once only' bottlings — once drunk,
gone forever!

THE KEEPERS OF THE QUAICH

THE Keepers of the Quaich is an exclusive society established by the Scotch whisky industry to honour those around the world who have contributed greatly to the standing and success of Scotch whisky.

It also aims to build on the value and prestige of Scotch whisky internationally and to further interest in the lesser known aspects and attributes of the 'Spirits of Scotland'.

The organisation has members from 38 countries and includes leaders of the Scotch whisky industry and noted Scotch whisky connoisseurs and characters. All have one fundamental link in common — a love of Scotland and Scotch whisky. Under the patronage of (among others) His Grace, The Duke of Atholl, banquets are regularly held at Blair Castle in Perthshire to invest new members as Keepers and to promote not only Scotch but also Scotland. The seal of the society is therefore most appropriate — bestowed by the Lord Lyon, it proclaims UISGEBEATHA GU BRATH — Water of Life Forever.

FOUNDING PARTNERS

United Distillers
33 Ellersly Road
EDINBURGH EH12 6JW
United Distillers, the spirits company of Guiness plc, is the major producer of branded spirits in the UK with a portfolio of over 100 brands of Scotch whisky, gin, vodka and bourbon. UK sales are the responsibility of Perth-based United Distillers (UK) Ltd.

Allied Distillers Ltd
2 Glasgow Road
DUMBARTON G82 1ND
Incorporating George Ballantine & Son, William Teacher & Sons and Stewart & Son of Dundee this new company formed in January 1988 focuses the inter-related whisky interests of Hiram Walker-Allied Vintners, the wines and spirits arm of Allied-Lyons plc. Headquartered in Dumbarton where the parent company operates the largest grain whisky distillery in Scotland, the new company continues an association with the town first started in 1938 by Hiram Walker.

Justerini & Brooks Ltd
151 Marylebone Road
LONDON NW1 5QE

This company was founded in 1749 by Giacomo Justerini, an Italian cordial maker who came to London in pursuit of an Opera singer. He failed in his quest for the lady, but remained to form a commercial alliance with George Johnson and together they set themselves up as wine merchants. By 1760 the company had been granted the first of its eight successive Royal Warrants and in 1830 the company was bought by Alfred Brooks. A century later the house brand of Scotch — J&B Rare dominated the company's exports to the United States. After merging with Twiss Brownings and Hallowes to form United Wine Traders, the company bought Gilbeys in 1962 to form International Distillers and Vintners, now the drinks division of Grand Metropolitan.

The Highland Distilleries Co plc
& Robertson & Baxter Ltd
106 West Nile Street
GLASGOW G1 2QY

The Highland Distilleries Company was incorporated in July 1887 as distillers of high quality malt whisky for the blending trade having secured the ownership of both Glenrothes and Bunnahabhain distilleries. Having acquired Glenglassaugh distillery in 1892 and Tamdhu in 1898, the company expanded its interests and later formed a close association with whisky brokers Robertson & Baxter Ltd. The malt portfolio was enlarged with the addition of Highland Park in Orkney in 1937 and its blended whisky interests were also furthered with the takeover of Matthew Gloag & Son Ltd, the Perth blenders of The Famous Grouse in 1970.

The Chivas & Glenlivet Division
111 Renfrew Road
PAISLEY PA3 4DY

In 1801 William Edward set up in business in Aberdeen as a wine and spirit merchant and grocer; he was joined some years later by James Chivas. They introduced Chivas Regal in the 1890's and this established their reputation within the trade. In 1949, Chivas Bros joined forces with Seagram's of Canada thus securing entry into the distilling world whilst strengthening their position in the trade. In 1950, they purchased Strathisla Distillery and in 1957 Glen Keith was built. In the 1970's, Chivas commissioned two further distilleries — Braes of Glenlivet and Allt a Bhainne. In 1978, Glenlivet Distillers joined the fold bringing four more distilleries into the portfolio - Glenlivet, Longmorn, Benriach and Caperdonich. The division is today responsible for all production, business development and global strategic planning for Seagram's Scotch whisky brands.

CORPORATE MEMBERS

Berry Bros & Rudd Ltd
3 St James's Street
LONDON SW1A 1EG

Burns Stewart
Distillers PLC
65 Kelburn Street
GLASGOW G78 1LD

Campbell Distillers Ltd
West Byrehill
KILWINNING KA13 6LE

Findlater Mackie Todd & Co Ltd
Deer Park Road
Merton Abbey
LONDON SW19 3TU

J&G Grant
Glenfarclas Distillery
Marypark
BALLINDALLOCH
Banffshire AB3 9BD

William Grant & Sons Ltd
Independence House
84 Lower Mortlake Road
RICHMOND
Surrey TW9 2HS

Invergordon Distillers
Group PLC
9-21 Salamander Place
EDINBURGH EH6 7JL

Inver House Distillers Ltd
Towers Road
AIRDRIE ML6 8PL

William Lawson
Distillers Ltd
288 Main Street
COATBRIDGE
ML5 3RH

Macallan Glenlivet Plc
CRAIGELLACHIE
Banffshire AB3 9RX

Macdonald Martin
Distillers Plc
186 Commercial Street
Leith
EDINBURGH EH6 6NN

Morrison Bowmore
Distillers Ltd
Springburn Bond
Carlisle Street
GLASGOW G21 1EQ

The North British
Distillery Co Ltd
Wheatfield Road
EDINBURGH
EH11 2PX

The Tomatin Distillery
Co Ltd
TOMATIN IV13 7YT

The Whyte & Mackay
Group PLC
Dalmore House
St Vincent Street
GLASGOW G2 5RG

INDEX

1 BENROMACH ✓
  COLEBURN (GOT c/H)
  CONVALMORE (GOT c/H
  DALLAS DHU (GOT)
2 GLENALLACHIE ✓
  GLEN ALBYN (GOT c/
  GLEN MHOR (GOT)
  MILLBURN (GOT)
3 BANFF ✓
4 GLEN ESK
5 GLENUGIE ✓
  GLENURY ROYAL (GOT)
  NORTH PORT (GOT)
  GLENLOCHY (GOT c/H
  GLENGRAIG
  GLENBURGIE
  ~~MILTON DUFF 1963~~